Material Adverse Change

Founded in 1807, John Wiley & Sons is the oldest independent publishing company in the United States. With offices in North America, Europe, Australia and Asia, Wiley is globally committed to developing and marketing print and electronic products and services for our customers' professional and personal knowledge and understanding.

The Wiley Finance series contains books written specifically for finance and investment professionals as well as sophisticated individual investors and their financial advisors. Book topics range from portfolio management to e-commerce, risk management, financial engineering, valuation and financial instrument analysis, as well as much more.

For a list of available titles, visit our Web site at www.WileyFinance .com.

Material Adverse Change

Lessons from Failed M&As

ROBERT V. STEFANOWSKI

WILEY

Published by John Wiley & Sons, Inc., Hoboken, New Jersey.

Published simultaneously in Canada.

For general information on our other products and services or for technical support, please contact our Customer Care Department within the United States at (800) 762–2974, outside the United States at (317) 572–3993, or fax (317) 572–4002.

Wiley publishes in a variety of print and electronic formats and by print-on-demand. Some material included with standard print versions of this book may not be included in e-books or in print-on-demand. If this book refers to media such as a CD or DVD that is not included in the version you purchased, you may download this material at http://booksupport.wiley.com. For more information about Wiley products, visit www.wiley.com.

Library of Congress Cataloging-in-Publication Data

Names: Stefanowski, Robert, author.
Title: Material adverse change : lessons from failed M&As / by Robert V.
  Stefanowski.
Description: Hoboken, New Jersey : John Wiley & Sons, Inc., [2018] | Includes
  index. |
Identifiers: LCCN 2017049041 (print) | LCCN 2017050859 (ebook) | ISBN
  9781118222430 (pdf) | ISBN 9781118236383 (epub) | ISBN 9781118066898
  (cloth)
Subjects: LCSH: Consolidation and merger of corporations—United States.
Classification: LCC HD2746.55.U5 (ebook) | LCC HD2746.55.U5 S74 2018 (print)
  | DDC 658.1/620973—dc23
LC record available at https://lccn.loc.gov/2017049041

Cover Design: Wiley
Cover Image: © peeterv/Getty Images

Printed in the United States of America

10 9 8 7 6 5 4 3 2 1

For my mom, I miss you.

Contents

Introduction: The Risks and Opportunities of Doing a Deal   xi

CHAPTER 1

Why Bad Deals Happen   1

A Practical Approach to Mergers and Acquisitions   3
A Case Study: RBS Buys ABN AMRO   4
Motivations for Deals   5
A Case Study: Bank of America Buys Merrill Lynch   5
Using M&A to Divert Attention   12
Using M&A to Grow Quickly   12
Using M&A to Solve Problems   13
Horizontal and Vertical Mergers   14
Conclusion   16

CHAPTER 2

Buy or Build?   19

A Case Study: Commerce Bank   21
A Case Study: Metro Bank   26
Is There Anything in Between?   29
A Case Study: Dow Corning Joint Venture   31
A Case Study: Bucknell Industries   32
Conclusion   34

CHAPTER 3

Let the Buyer Beware   37

Wachovia Buys Golden West   40
AOL Time Warner Merger   46
Wells Fargo Buys Wachovia   48

CHAPTER 4

The Opportunities and Risks of Expanding Your Business Globally   51

Telenor India Joint Venture   54
Telenor's Global Strategy over Time   56

Telenor Expands into Eastern Europe   57
Telenor Pushes into Asia   59
The Telenor Unitech Joint Venture   61
Postmortem on the Telenor Unitech Joint Venture   63
Lessons Learned   64
Trends for the Future   67

CHAPTER 5
Culture Is Critical   **69**
A Case Study from China   71
A Case Study from Japan   74
A Summary of Other Best Practices   76

CHAPTER 6
Who Is Behind the Curtain?   **85**
A Case Study: Lloyds HBOS   87
A Case Study: Kraft Buys Cadbury   96

CHAPTER 7
Is It Too Late to Back Out?   **103**
Case Study One: Bank of America Purchases Merrill Lynch   106
Case Study Two: AT&T/T Mobile   110
Case Study Three: Verizon Bids for Yahoo   115
Conclusion   116

CHAPTER 8
How to Negotiate a Better Deal   **119**
Ten Best Practices for Effective Negotiation   124

CHAPTER 9
Making It Right   **135**
Background   137
Be Strategic   138
Maintain a Rational Organizational Structure   140
Structure the Deal Properly   141
Recognize the Importance of Brand   142
Efficient Distribution   143
Beware of Culture   144
Have Financing Lined Up in Advance   145
Establish an Appropriate M&A Approval Process   145
Integrate Early and Often   146
Clear Legal and Regulatory Process   146

Don't Overpay 147
Continuous Learning 148
A Case Study: J.P. Morgan Buys Bear Stearns 148
Conclusion 152

CHAPTER 10
Where Do We Go from Here? **155**
How Fast We Forget 157

APPENDIX A
Trinity International/American Public Media Group: Material Adverse
Change Clause **169**

APPENDIX B
Bank of America/Merrill: Material Adverse Change Clause **171**

About the Author **175**

Index **177**

Introduction: The Risks and Opportunities of Doing a Deal

Did any board member suggest that Bank of America should go ahead and invoke the MAC?

No, not at that point ... most people thought the severity of the reaction meant that they (i.e., U.S. Federal Reserve and Treasury) firmly believed it was systemic risk.

—Ken Lewis, former chairman and CEO of Bank of America
during U.S. Attorney Deposition on Executive
Compensation
February 26, 2009[1]

On October 8, 2002, Fred Goodwin, then CEO of Royal Bank of Scotland (RBS), outbid Bob Diamond, the head of Barclays Capital, to conclude his long quest to purchase ABN AMRO Bank for $96.5 billion. Goodwin had built RBS from a small regional bank to a global powerhouse that was one of the largest banks in the world. For his efforts, Goodwin was voted "Businessman of the Year" by *Forbes* magazine in 2002. He had earned the name "Fred the Shred" for his ability to ruthlessly take out people while reducing the cost of operating the companies he acquired. *Forbes* proclaimed, "In a tough era for lenders, Fred Goodwin has built his bank into the world's fifth largest with a market cap of $70 billion."[2] Goodwin had a pragmatic approach to acquisitions, leveraging his instinct and experience running businesses to buy and transform companies.

Five years later, this jewel of an acquisition did not live up to expectations. Credit losses in the ABN loan book, key employee departures, an inability to integrate the complex ABN AMRO computer systems, and an overall downturn in the economy drove RBS's stock price from a high of over £7.00 per share ($4.2 per share) to a low of less than 50 pence per share (31 cents per share). Material adverse events in the company proved that a purchase price of close to $100 billion was more than ABN AMRO was truly worth.

With the continued deterioration of the economy and the rising of a Great Recession, the issues surrounding this deal became more and more apparent. Indeed, by the time of the depths of the recession in December 2007, for the *same* $100 billion that RBS used to buy ABN AMRO, an investor could have purchased *100 percent* of Goldman Sachs, RBS, General Motors, Citibank, Deutsche Bank, *and* Merrill Lynch all together.[3]

What Can You Get for $100 Billion?

General Motors	$ 1 billion
Deutsche Bank	$25 billion
Goldman Sachs	$36 billion
Citibank	$ 8 billion
RBS	$12 billion
Total	**$82 billion**

Despite his best intentions and a desire to enhance the value to RBS shareholders by purchasing an exciting new business, this unfortunate acquisition cost Fred Goodwin his job. Thousands of shareholders who had invested in RBS stock lost all of their value. Goodwin was summarily dismissed from RBS, villainized by the press, and received threats on his personal safety. He was forced to leave his home and retreat to a friend's Majorcan Villa to avoid the press and an angry public. It was not until May 2016, over eight years after the fateful acquisition, that Goodwin was finally cleared of all criminal charges relative to the RBS deal.

This book is not intended to cast blame on CEOs, investment bankers, or other advisors unfortunate enough to be involved in failed transactions. I have found these constituencies to be hardworking and largely interested in the success of the companies they work for. Rather, it is to probe why deals don't work and the risks implicit in major transactions such as RBS paying close to $100 billion to purchase ABN AMRO. Through a review of past failures and the reasons behind these failures, we can better anticipate the potential pitfalls of future deals and avoid the disruption to a company and destruction of wealth to shareholders when deals don't work.

In the mergers and acquisitions (M&A) profession, due diligence is defined as the work accountants, lawyers, human resources, risk departments, senior executives, and other key personnel of the buyer complete prior to agreeing to purchase a company. Take the analogy of a newly married couple who wish to buy their first house; we will call them the "Wilsons." The Wilsons typically look through the real estate listings, talk to a realtor, visit several properties, and narrow the search down to one house. At this point they will do a more detailed review of the property, looking for areas that may be damaged and in need of repair or replacement, or areas that the seller should correct before he sells the house. The Wilsons will likely hire outside experts such as an inspector to examine the house, an appraiser to verify the home's market value, a lawyer to help negotiate terms, and so forth. In essence, the Wilsons will want to be more than comfortable with the home before they commit money to purchase it.

Similarly, in successful acquisitions, a corporate or financial buyer of a company will analyze the financial position of the target, meet with key management, review the operations, update the company's financial projections, and investigate legal liabilities, all to determine if the company is worth the price being paid. Deal teams will hire consultants, lawyers, and accountants to help them with this process. Once complete, the buyer will sign a contract to purchase the company at a specified price over a certain time period.

In larger M&A deals, there is normally a time period between actual agreement to purchase (*signing*) and the completion of the transaction (*closing*). This time is used to satisfy contingencies such as government approval for the deal to happen, shareholder consents, employee union agreements, or agreements from other parties who need to consent to the transaction. Once all of these have been satisfied, the buyer and seller will move toward final closing of the transaction. It can take months to close a deal after contracts have been signed. This time between signing and closing is one of the most risky parts of the entire M&A process.

Take the example of the Wilsons, who now own the perfect home (as a result of completing very good due diligence!) and decide they need a car to go with it. They decide to buy a used car to save money and enter into a contract to purchase the car on Monday (signing). During the week they will withdraw the cash, arrange for financing and insurance, and then pay for and take possession of the car on Friday (closing). The Wilsons will absolutely want the car to be in the same condition on Friday that it was on Monday when they agreed to purchase it. But what if the owner decided to drive across the country from Tuesday to Thursday? What if the car was in an accident on Wednesday? Clearly the Wilsons will want some protection that the car will be in the same condition on Friday as it was when they agreed to purchase it on Monday if not to be able to walk away from the purchase.

Buyers in the M&A world face the same challenges. The target continues to function between signing and closing and is subject to the external risks of the business, the economy, and other acts beyond its control. Therefore, a buyer is at risk as they have agreed to purchase the company at signing, but the existing management team continues to run the company on a daily basis, hopefully well, for the buyer. A legal clause referred to as a *material adverse change* (MAC) has been crafted by attorneys to protect the buyer during this period between signing and closing.

An MAC allows the buyer to walk away from the deal if the target does not continue to run the company effectively or the firm incurs material changes that make the company less valuable. Attorneys have made the

MAC clause much more complicated over the years. For example, years ago MAC clauses allowed buyers to walk away from transactions for the occurrence of natural disasters, acts of war, or terrorism. Unfortunately, due to the turmoil in the world since then, such events are no longer infrequent and these are no longer legitimate reasons for a buyer to walk away from a deal. But the concept remains the same. The buyer can back out of the deal if certain other bad things happen between signing and closing

The combination of due diligence and an MAC provision sounds perfect. In theory, the buyer gets to spend as much time as they want reviewing the corporate records; meeting with key employees; understanding the legal, environmental, and risk issues; and gaining an overall comfort with the target operations before agreeing to the purchase. Further, the MAC clause allows the buyer to walk away if material unusual events occur *after* they have agreed to buy in concept, but *before* they make final payment.

But many CEOs of major corporations do not exercise these rights as buyers or do enough due diligence to fully understand what they bought. Whether it is RBS's purchase of ABN AMRO or Bank of America's purchase of Merrill Lynch, these mistakes can have dramatic impacts for their company, their shareholders, and their careers. But bad deals continue to happen time after time. What are the factors motivating CEOs to put their careers on the line to acquire large companies? Why does this continue to happen despite highly publicized acquisition failures and the potential civil and criminal liability for the individuals involved? Why are successful companies not satisfied with where they are, pursuing a logical and orderly method of organic growth to improve their performance?

This book attempts to answer these questions. Whether you are a corporate CEO, an investment banker directly involved in M&A, an attorney, a human resources executive, a CFO, or a casual reader of business books, it will provide guidance on how to avoid these mistakes going forward. Landmark M&A case studies, such as Bank of America's purchase of Merrill Lynch and Kraft's purchase of Cadbury, will be used to answer these questions and provide hard evidence as to why these errors that defy common sense continue to be committed by well-established, successful, and highly intelligent businesspeople.

NOTES

1. U.S. Legal Support Inc., Examination of Kenneth Lewis, taken at the State of New York of the Attorney General, February 26, 2009.
2. *Forbes*, December 22, 2002.
3. Based on total market capitalization of the firms as of 12/31/08 as listed in Fact Set.

Material Adverse Change

CHAPTER 1

Why Bad Deals Happen

This really is a merger of equals. I wouldn't have come back to work for anything less than this fantastic opportunity. This lets me combine my two great loves—technology and biscuits.
— Lou Gerstner, former chairman and CEO, IBM,
commenting on Cisco's proposed acquisition
of Nabisco from Kraft Foods

A PRACTICAL APPROACH TO MERGERS AND ACQUISITIONS

What do you look for when deciding on a bank to deposit your money? Given the recent large bank failures, the financial strength of the bank is certainly one main consideration. You may also be interested in the bank's customer service, checking account options, hours of operation, and so on. More financially experienced individuals will try to find the bank with the highest interest rates paid on customer deposits. For the most part, choosing a bank is a purely fact-based, rational decision.

Now assume that you are the CEO of a global company and are trying to decide what company to buy. Criteria will include the company strategy, quality of personnel, and of course the rate of return and profit you can earn. So it should be easy. Rank the companies for sale by their level of return and pick the highest one. For those of you who took business in college, remember the concept of net present value? You calculate the expected cash flows of the company and discount them by your firm's weighted average cost of capital. The project with the highest internal rate of return[1] (IRR) is the one you choose.

Many of the university students I teach assume that this simple, scientific, and straightforward approach is how it works in the real world. This is the way the math works. This is how it was explained in the college corporate finance classes.

My professor is a brilliant person—it must be right. It takes a long time to convince students that the real world is much more complicated than this. Subjective judgments, personal agendas, egos, and a whole host of other human emotions often have more impact on these decisions than the pure numbers suggest.

In my experience, a purely academic approach to mergers and acquisitions is rarely the best way to make a decision. For example, an absolute comparison of returns versus cost of capital may have been a primary driver at the start of Royal Bank of Scotland's (RBS's) process to purchase ABN AMRO. However, as the auction went along and competition for ABN intensified between RBS and Barclays bank, it became less about the numbers and more about the softer items such as each firm's reputation, the impact to stock price of winning or losing the auction, public perception of the deal, and the attitudes of employees and customers.

A CASE STUDY: RBS BUYS ABN AMRO

Many postmortems have been written on Fred Goodwin's relentless pursuit of ABN AMRO. Early in the process, several internal and external RBS constituencies began to question the true motivations around this acquisition. One RBS analyst said at the time, "Some of our investors think Sir Fred is a megalomaniac who cares more about size than shareholder value."[2] But either these concerns never filtered up to the boardroom or, more likely, they were discussed and discounted; the momentum of a deal and commitment toward closing can often override very legitimate issues.

It must have been difficult to justify the ultimate purchase price of $96.5 billion when the initial bid from RBS in March 2008 was $92.4 billion. Did the fundamental operations and value of ABN AMRO improve by over $4.0 billion in the span of six months? In reality, a combination of poor integration, unrealistic projections, and a softening economy drove a significant *loss* in the value of ABN operations during this six-month period, and the price should have gone down, not up. An RBS trader commented at the time that "once you started to look around ABN's trading books, you realized that a lot of their businesses, where valuations were based on assumptions, were based on forecasts that were super-aggressive."[3]

In hindsight, losing this deal may be the best thing that ever happened to Barclays and the CEO of Barclays Capital Bob Diamond. RBS never recovered from difficulty in integrating ABN AMRO, the poor asset quality, and the massive losses it incurred. In June 2007, RBS raised £12 billion of capital by issuing new shares in a rights offering to try to save the company from the massive overpayment and operating losses resulting from the ABN acquisition. At the time, this rights offering was the largest fundraising in the history of the British public equity markets; however, it still proved to be insufficient.

News of the serious issues associated with the acquisition of ABN was leaking to the market and the firm's capitalization decreased by more than a quarter—more than the total amount of capital raised by the rights offering itself. By October 7, 2008, RBS, its management team, its shareholders, and the U.K. government all realized that it was too late. The U.K. Treasury Select Committee started to provide emergency liquidity to RBS; in effect U.K. taxpayers were becoming the major shareholders in the new RBS.

In contrast, Barclays went on to be very successful. The bank has had some more recent issues, but Barclays had a strong enough balance sheet to withstand the Great Recession without bailout support from the government. Bob Diamond was ultimately promoted from the head of Barclays Capital to succeed John Varley as the head of the entire bank. While Diamond was dismissed from his post in 2012 for issues related to the LIBOR scandal, he was fortunate enough to have prolonged his tenure at Barclays by avoiding a disaster deal in ABN. In the world of M&A, winning the deal is not always the best outcome. The party that wins a competitive auction for a company is normally the party that is willing to pay the most! While this works out fantastically in some cases, it can cause problems for the buyers. As we saw with RBS, winning a deal may be the biggest curse of all.

MOTIVATIONS FOR DEALS

RBS's purchase of ABN AMRO seems truly illogical in hindsight. So why did it happen? Simple human nature is involved in all of these deals. It is easy to lose perspective, to forget the facts, and to become emotionally vested in the purchase. Many people can sympathize with this phenomenon. Have you ever paid more than you should have for a new home, a car, or a designer handbag because you became emotionally invested and just had to have it? Marketers all over the world depend on this human trait to sell product. As we see time and time again, it is no different in the "scientific" world of corporate finance.

Many CEOs are "Type A" personalities who like being in charge and enjoy the spotlight of the press. The battle for ABN was covered daily in the national press. While not intentional, it could be that the competitive nature of each CEO had as much to do with the rising price for ABN as the detailed acquisition models used to derive a fair price. In fact, by the time the purchase price rose to $96.5 billion, I imagine that the internal rate of return of the escalating bids for ABN AMRO was largely ignored while many of the softer issues were driving the ultimate decision.

A CASE STUDY: BANK OF AMERICA BUYS MERRILL LYNCH

The merger between Bank of America (BofA) and Merrill Lynch in September 2008 is another high-profile example of this phenomenon. Bank of America, headquartered in Charlotte, North Carolina, operated retail bank branches throughout the United States and the rest of the world. Originally founded in 1904, BofA had grown to be the largest retail bank in the United States.

Ken Lewis grew up in the southern United States, graduated from Georgia State University, and joined North Carolina National Bank in 1969. He became CEO of the successor organization, Bank of America, in 2001 upon the retirement of Hugh McColl. Lewis was admired for his strategic vision, execution of acquisitions, and ability to improve the operations of companies he acquired. By the mid-1990s, BofA had become a premier retail bank and Lewis was awarded "Banker of the Year" by *American Banker* in 2008 (*American Banker*, October 2008).

However, as a retail bank based in the southern United States, BofA did not have the prestigious reputation of the high-powered investment banks on Wall Street that were advising on multibillion-dollar acquisitions. Although widely respected, BofA was a large retail bank that took in consumer and corporate deposits and lent them out for car loans, home mortgages, leveraged loans, and other financing to individuals and corporations. BofA was headquartered in North Carolina, not New York City. Their core business was not as sexy as the billion-dollar transactions and initial public offerings being negotiated by investment banks making millions of dollars in fees for their firms and for themselves. While Lewis ran a first-class organization in its own right, it was and would always be considered second-tier to the global investment banks on Wall Street.

Merrill Lynch was a venerable investment bank on Wall Street with a heritage dating back to the early twentieth century. Founded by Charles Merrill and Edmund Lynch, Merrill became one of the leading providers of wealth management, securities, trading, corporate finance, and investment banking. The reputation Merrill held was very different from that of BofA. As a full-service investment bank headquartered on Wall Street, Merrill was absolutely included in the Wall Street elite. Over the years, Merrill's investment bank directed some of the largest and most visible transactions in the world of global financial services. Merrill's equity division had taken some of the most famous companies in the world public via initial public offerings. Merrill was able to attract the best recruits out of top colleges while improving the quality of management by tempting senior players from other Wall Street firms with employment contracts worth tens of millions of dollars.

In the late 2000s, Merrill decided to quickly expand its mortgage operations via internal growth and the acquisition of 12 major mortgage originators. The number of mortgage loans had exploded with the continued rise in the U.S. housing market. Merrill viewed mortgage lending as a way to diversify from its core M&A and equity underwriting business and bring in new revenue streams. A large part of this mortgage business included "subprime" mortgages, or mortgages made to borrowers with poor credit histories. These loans were attractive to Merrill because the bank could charge these customers a higher interest rate. Some of these borrowers had nowhere else to go and had to pay higher rates to secure financing. Many banks were worried about lending to these customers who had not paid back other loans, or historically paid loans late, resulting in a poor credit rating. However by 2006, over 20 percent of mortgage loans were to consumers considered to be subprime.

To manage exposure and generate fee income, the mortgages were packaged together into a pool and *securitized* to other investors. In other words, hundreds of mortgages were grouped into one pool of assets. Individual securities were then created that represented a percentage ownership in this broad pool of mortgages. An investor in one of these securities held a fraction ownership in the entire pool, enabling the investor to share in the risks and rewards of owning mortgage loans.

Financial professionals spoke about a "new paradigm" of risk. No one bank held the liability for the entire pool of mortgages any more. Rather, ownership of the individual securities was distributed among hundreds, if not thousands, of individual investors all over the world. The new theory was that if the pool of assets went bad and the mortgages were not repaid, it would not be a major global economic problem because the risk for any individual security holder was small. This eliminated the *systematic* risk posed by large borrowings to subprime mortgage holders held by one large bank because the securities were distributed in smaller sizes to multiple investors.

Securitization of mortgages became a massive business on Wall Street. Investment banks earned large fees by originating these loans or purchasing them from other borrowers and selling off the securities to others in the secondary market. Securitizations for other types of loans soon surfaced, such as automobile loans, corporate loans, credit card debt, and so on. These securities were called collateralized debt obligations (CDOs) or collateralized loan obligations (CLOs), depending on the type of loan pool.

As the global housing market boomed, banks started to lend more and more aggressively to weaker credits. This created more residential loans to supply the insatiable demand in the CDO market. It got to the point where "liar loans" were created that allowed individuals to take out home mortgages with no written evidence at all. In other words, a homebuyer could walk into a bank and list his net worth, level of income, and ability to pay back the mortgage. The mortgage broker would ask a few questions, but not require *any* documentation supporting the representations of the applicant. They trusted the applicant to not lie about his financial position.

Lenders started to loan up to 110 percent of a home's market value (i.e., more than the home was worth when the loan was taken out). This allowed a buyer to purchase a home without any of her own money committed. To make matters worse, the homeowner then received another 10 percent in addition to this amount and was allowed to keep the cash. The bank's theory was that home prices never came down. Given the escalation in home values, the loan would be worth more than the mortgage again after several months when the always-rising home prices would make the loan secure over time. This had become a very profitable business for Merrill Lynch and others on Wall Street.

All of this worked well until the housing bubble burst in late 2006. Individuals were no longer able to afford the significant mortgage payments they had signed up for in the boom years. The stock of homes for sale and foreclosed homes grew exponentially, further driving down values. As a result, banks holding large portfolios of subprime CDO assets started to incur defaults on their payments as the quality of the loan portfolios plummeted. As one of the largest holders of subprime assets, Merrill Lynch was hit particularly hard by the abrupt change in the economy. In October 2007, Merrill Lynch announced a $7.9 billion write-down resulting from exposure to CDOs. This produced Merrill's largest quarterly loss, $2.3 billion, in the history of the firm.

As a result of this crisis, CEO Stan O'Neal was replaced by John Thain, then CEO of the New York Stock Exchange, in October 2007. With an MIT and Harvard education and a prior job as president and co–chief operating officer of Goldman Sachs, Thain was the quintessential Wall Street executive, a stark contrast to Ken Lewis, the southern, state university–educated retail banking head based in North Carolina.

Earlier in 2007, the U.S. economy had suffered several severe shocks. Bear Stearns was a global investment bank founded in 1923. In March 2008, the Federal Reserve Bank of New York provided an emergency loan to try to save Bear from losses stemming from its own CDO business. However, the company could not be saved and was sold to JP Morgan Chase for $10 per share. This was up from the original offer from JP Morgan Chase of $2 per share, but still sharply below Bear's 52-week-high share price of $133. The Federal Reserve also guaranteed up to $30 billion of troubled mortgage and all other assets that got Bear Stearns into trouble.

In mid-September, the U.S. Federal Reserve had to step in and bail out yet another Wall Street firm. This time it was American International Group (AIG), with an $85 billion credit facility that entitled the U.S. government to a 79.9 percent equity ownership in the company. AIG also had a distinguished history. An insurance company and bank founded in 1919 with more than 88 million customers in 130 countries, by 2000 AIG was listed as the twenty-ninth largest public company in the world. The fall of AIG was set in motion by a credit downgrade for the company from AAA to AA. This caused counterparties to various complex financial instruments to insist on AIG posting additional collateral or settling the contract immediately. AIG did not have sufficient cash capacity to deal with all of these contracts at once, resulting in the need for an emergency loan from the U.S. government.

Finally on the weekend of September 12, 2002, this sequence of severe economic events came to a head. Lehman Brothers was the next largest Wall Street firm on the brink of bankruptcy due to massive losses in the existing portfolio. Founded in 1850, Lehman had grown to be the fourth largest investment bank in the United States behind only Goldman Sachs, Morgan Stanley, and Merrill Lynch. With over 26,000 employees, a Lehman failure would add considerable systematic risk to an already fragile economy.

However, the Federal Reserve had seen enough. They were concerned about the moral hazard of continuing to bail out financial institutions that had taken imprudent amounts of risk. If bankers were confident that the government would always bail them out for mistakes, there was incentive to take as much risk as possible. If the risks turned out well, bankers would be handsomely rewarded. If the trades went bad, the government would step in to pick up the losses. The banks could not lose, no matter how aggressive they became. The U.S. Federal Reserve believed that they had to set a precedent. They had to show Wall Street banks that executives were going to start taking accountability for their mistakes—both for their banks and for themselves.

By Friday, September 12, 2008, most expected that Lehman would not have enough cash to open for business on Monday morning. At 6:00 P.M. on Friday evening, an emergency meeting was called for the most powerful CEOs on Wall Street at the Federal Reserve Building in New York. The government urged these bank leaders to find a solution to prevent a potential global economic meltdown on Monday morning if Lehman did not open its doors. Each CEO claimed that their bank was not at fault for the problems encountered by Lehman, and they could not justify spending their own shareholders' money to bail out a competitor. The government stressed that it was in the best interest of the shareholders of all banks in the room to stabilize the U.S. economy as soon as possible.

Negotiations continued throughout the weekend, but no solutions emerged. With the possibility of a Lehman Brothers' bankruptcy growing more likely by the minute, Merrill became worried about its own survival. At 6:30 A.M. on Saturday morning, John Thain received a call from his COO suggesting they call Ken Lewis at Bank of America for help. Thain initially resisted. He insisted that Merrill could survive as an independent bank if they could sell off non-core assets to raise cash quickly. However, as discussions continued through Saturday morning, Thain relented and asked for a meeting with Ken Lewis. But he could not bring himself to make the call to Lewis personally. After pressure from his legal counsel, Thain again relented and agreed to make the call to Lewis directly.

Lewis immediately traveled to New York City and met Thain at the BofA corporate apartment in the Time Warner Center. Thain opened the conversation bluntly: "I'd like to explore whether you would have an interest in buying 9.9 percent of our company and providing a large liquidity facility."[4] Lewis countered that he was not really interested in buying 9.9 percent of the company—he wanted to buy the whole bank.

Negotiations became tense. As the day progressed, it became apparent that the only way discussions would proceed would be if BofA were allowed to buy 100 percent of Merrill. BofA initially took the position that they needed $70 billion in government guarantees to proceed with the purchase. They did not have time to adequately assess the assets over the weekend. They were being pushed by the government to close before Monday morning to avoid economic chaos. Merrill Lynch insisted on a purchase price of $30 per share. At 8:00 A.M. on Sunday, Thain and Lewis met again. Thain tried to make the case for a high valuation of Merrill, despite the fact that Merrill's stock price was in a downward spiral.

As Sunday went on, the pressure from the government to do a deal continued to increase. Thain became more and more concerned that Merrill would not survive the next week without a deal in some form. The balance of negotiating power was slowly moving from Merrill to BofA. Late on Sunday, BofA agreed to $29 per share for Merrill stock. This was equivalent to a 70 percent premium over Merrill's stock closing price on Friday. Further, the federal government refused to provide any support to backstop failed assets. BofA shareholders were taking 100 percent of the risk associated with the Merrill portfolio while paying a 70 percent premium to the market value of the company!

The deal was announced on Monday, September 15. BofA agreed to purchase Merrill for approximately $50 billion with each Merrill shareholder receiving .8595 shares of BofA stock for each share of Merrill they held. BofA shares immediately fell 21 percent on the announcement, and Merrill's shares rose to $17 per share, still a massive discount to the amount BofA had agreed to pay. Clearly, the market was not a big fan of this deal. While Thain had saved his company, Lewis had entered into a huge transaction with many unknown risks that put his own shareholders in danger. As we will see later in this book, the ultimate outcome of the transaction was materially worse than the negative market sentiment on that Monday.

So why did Lewis go forward with the deal? Unlike his highly levered peers on Wall Street, BofA was in very good condition relative to the rest of the market in this unstable environment. As investment banks only, Merrill, AIG, and Bear Stearns relied purely on the capital markets for funding. When this capital dried up along with the economy, they had nowhere to turn other than the federal government. Alternatively, BofA had a huge retail base to fall back on. Retail and corporate deposits at the bank provided BofA with billions of dollars of liquidity to wait out the financial crisis.

Lewis forged ahead. He effectively had one weekend to complete due diligence on a massively complicated, global investment bank. He put himself, his company, and his shareholders at a massive risk. What was driving Lewis forward? Had he lost his perspective? Was Lewis trying to protect the global economy? Or did he actually think that the troubled Merrill operations were worth $50 billion?

BofA's purchase of Merrill is a perfect example of the nonscientific reasons often causing two parties to enter into a deal. It was not about the financial returns on the deal. It was not about ranking the companies available for sale from highest expected returns to the lowest and picking the best one. I would argue that the purchase was much more about the softer issues around strategy, status, and growth. If the decision were purely numbers-based, it is hard to believe that Ken Lewis and the BofA board of directors would agree to spend $50 billion to purchase Merrill Lynch between a Friday afternoon and Monday morning. How on earth was Bank of America able to analyze an organization with 288,000 employees, 57 million customers, and operations in 41 countries from the close of business on Friday to Monday morning? Yet it happened.

To make matters worse, BofA's agreement to purchase Merrill was signed on September 15, 2008, with an anticipated closing date of December 31, 2008. This period between signing of the deal and closing is a very risky period for a buyer. The buyer has essentially committed to purchase the company, yet the existing management team continues to run it for the months up to closing. The buyer is on the hook for anything that management team decides to do during this transition period. For example, in the case of BofA/Merrill, John Thain and his people were promised multibillion-dollar bonus payments at the time the deal was signed under the assumption that Merrill would perform in line with management's financial projections for the year.

However, as we now know, several material changes in the business occurred during this 45-day period. The Great Recession brought the world's economy to its knees with companies as legendary as Goldman Sachs and Morgan Stanley worried about their own survival. Why would anyone in his right mind go through with this transaction given what happened to the world and to Merrill's performance? Despite this subpar performance, Thain accelerated approximately $4 billion in bonus payments to employees of Merrill just prior to the close of the deal to avoid having them canceled by BofA upon acquisition. This case raises some very difficult questions. Did Ken Lewis know that Thain was about to pay $4 billion of his shareholders' money to executives that had overseen the downfall of Merrill?

Further, was there no Material Adverse Change Clause in the contract that allowed Lewis and BofA to back away from the deal entirely after the economy collapsed? Did Lewis honestly believe that Merrill was still worth the $50 billion he agreed to pay on September 15, 2008, particularly given events after this time? Was the reputation of Lewis and BofA a factor in his decision to keep moving forward? Or were there external pressures from shareholders, employees, the U.S. government, or other stakeholders to proceed with a transaction that everyone knew was doomed to failure? As we will see later in the book, many of these questions can be answered not by cold, hard facts, but by human emotions and the actions of strong personalities.

USING M&A TO DIVERT ATTENTION

A diversion from the real issues is often another irrational reason for M&A. A large, highly visible deal can distract shareholders and analysts from the core issues facing a corporation. It is actually hard to believe that smart corporate senior managers would use this as an excuse to enter into a deal. But it happens.

Some have argued that Johnson & Johnson's 2011 takeover of Synthes was done for just this reason.[5] In April 2011, J&J had a problem. Between 2010 and 2011, over 50 drugs and devices J&J produced were recalled from the government due to questions surrounding their safety. Such popular drugs as Tylenol and Motrin had to be recalled due to mistakes in production. J&J's medical device division even had a recall on artificial hips. And many of these hips had already been implanted in patients.

While these problems were likely not the only motivation for the Synthes deal, the deal came at a good time to provide some positive news. Given the high visibility around product recalls, a large deal to distract the public was certainly not the worst thing that could have happened. One major shareholder stated, "J&J had a severe challenge to its premier reputation given all the recalls. This relatively bold step to buy a premier company is a significant move in the right direction."[6]

USING M&A TO GROW QUICKLY

A company's need to grow is certainly a far more rational reason to acquire. Global stock markets are putting increasing pressure on companies to expand quickly. A failure to meet a quarterly earnings forecast can significantly hurt the stock price. Economic pressures have resulted in declining margins, revenue reductions, and corresponding shortfalls in profit for many large corporations. It is very hard to compensate for these issues via "organic growth," that is, growing your company by doing more business through existing product lines and channels. Alternatively, M&A is an easy way to gain scale and grow earnings quickly.

Let's take Apple as an example. For the year ended December 31, 2015, Apple produced gross earnings of $53.4 billion and earnings per share of $9.22. Most companies need to grow at least 3 to 5 percent a year to show the progress needed to continue an improvement in their stock price. In the case of Apple, 5 percent of $53.4 billion is over $2.5 billion of incremental earnings. In other words, Apple needs to grow earnings by over $2.5 billion year after year to show the needed improvement in earnings per share. This is the equivalent of adding a company the entire size of Nike every year.

This kind of continued growth rate is very hard to do organically. Most world-class companies like Apple have already optimized their operations and realized significant market share. They can try to grow their markets by taking business from competitors, becoming more efficient on the cost side, introducing new products, or trying to increase margins. Although all of this is possible on the fringes, making immediate wholesale changes that are material enough to matter is difficult without a large acquisition.

Another way to stimulate revenue growth is by entering new markets or geographies. This is also very hard to do organically. But an acquisition can give you an immediate presence in new areas. This makes it extremely tempting to look at M&A as a way to grow, take some of the pressure off earnings, and improve share price. CEOs need to remain balanced and resist this pressure. Good deals that provide entry into new markets or products certainly make sense. However, pursuing M&A just for the sake of quick growth or to relieve shareholder pressure can be dangerous. While this might help in the short term, the issues with fundamentally bad deals will certainly surface in the medium to long term.

USING M&A TO SOLVE PROBLEMS

Assume that you are the head of Europe for a large U.S. financial services company. Your CEO has challenged you to establish a banking presence in Italy by the end of the year. In addition you are $25mm behind your net income target for the year with no real ideas on how to make up the shortfall.

One way to establish this presence would be to build it yourself. But let's consider what is involved to get it done this way. You would need to hire a complete team in Italy including salespeople, underwriters, a finance staff, and a CEO capable of building a business quickly. You would need to apply for a license to do banking in Italy. You would encounter numerous logistical issues as simple as finding a building for corporate headquarters and locations for local bank branches.

Alternatively, if you could find an Italian bank to buy, the process would be much easier. You would immediately have a banking license, employees, and a complete operation in Italy. You would get immediate scale rather than having to take the time to build it. And perhaps most importantly, you get immediate earnings by being able to add the earnings of the Italian bank going forward into your own earnings for the year.

Think about the terrific discussion you can have with your CEO at the end of the year after buying this Italian bank. You gained an immediate, credible, and established banking presence in the country he so desperately wanted you to enter. You have also solved your net income problem by being able to add the Italian bank's earnings into yours for the year. You have solved both of your challenges in one stroke of the pen. However, as we will see later in this book, it is never quite as easy as this. Further, as many smart CEOs have subsequently realized, the disastrous effects of doing a poor deal significantly outweigh the benefits that can be achieved in many cases.

This is why most successful firms have a very thorough corporate review process around buying companies. Each of a company's divisions normally has its own objectives for growth into new products and geographies along with very challenging net income targets. Left to their own devices, business units would likely ask for as much funding from corporate retained earnings as they can get. If they can attract more of this capital, they can grow their business more quickly. If they are starved of capital, it will be very hard to grow.

The job of most corporate senior management and boards is not about micromanaging the individual business units, but rather managing the amount of capital to allocate to each unit and for what purpose—in many cases to acquire. Unfortunately, the amount of capital for all businesses is not unlimited. Difficult choices must be made as to who gets this money.

Again, in a purely academic approach it would be easy. All the corporate board has to do is rank the projects from highest to lowest internal rate of return and allocate capital to the ones at the top. But it is not that simple. The overall corporate strategy, strategic goals of each unit, and the personalities of the persons heading the unit all factor into the equation. In many cases, the credibility of the person presenting the deal and the board's confidence in him is more important than a pure mathematical calculation of IRRs.

HORIZONTAL AND VERTICAL MERGERS

Horizontal and vertical combinations are another reason frequently cited for M&A. Horizontal mergers are where one competitor in an industry buys another. The classic example of horizontal mergers is the consolidation of U.S. banking institutions. Years ago, one could travel down any town center in America and see multiple bank branches. In my home state of Connecticut, it was a Fleet Bank branch office, next to a Union Trust branch, next to a New Haven Savings Bank, and so on. There was really no need for three different bank branches in the space of a quarter mile on the same street.

By combining branches the buyer could improve revenues while taking out cost. These impacts are referred to as *synergies*. The best way to describe synergies is $1 + 1 = 3$. Let's use the Connecticut banking example. Do customers really need three different bank branches within one-minute walking distance of each other on one city street? Certainly their needs could be met by one bank in the area with a branch large enough to accommodate local demand. A significant amount of cost can be taken out in such a consolidation. Real estate costs would be lowered by combining several branches into one facility. Staff numbers could be reduced as economies of scale are obtained by having all employees in one spot.

On the revenue side, sharing of customer lists and cross-selling products could drive incremental income once the banks have been combined. If managed properly, these cost and revenue synergies can be achieved at the same time that customers receive equal or better service. Such synergies are normally the main drivers to horizontal mergers.

A vertical acquisition is one where a company buys one of its supply chain providers. One example can be seen in the rise of coal-fired power plants in emerging markets. Severe shortages of power and other infrastructure limitations have started to impair the ability of the emerging economies to keep growing. Many privately held companies are starting to address this need with the building and renovation of significant power sources to supplement insufficient power generation from public utilities.

However, this extreme demand for power has driven the cost of coal up and, more importantly, limited supply. Power companies have spent significant amounts to build the power generation infrastructure with large fixed costs. They have large pools of workers on contract to work the equipment. These energy producers cannot afford to have the large plants remain idle due to a shortage of their primary raw material, coal.

As a result, major power producers are starting to buy their own coalmines, often in countries outside of their own where demand is less. This type of *vertical integration* helps ensure that the coal is ready and available to meet demand. The power company, not the coal vendor, now decides when, how much, and how to distribute coal to the plants for energy conversion. Perhaps most importantly, the owner of the power plant can much better anticipate the price he will have to pay for this coal. The cost to extract the coal from the mine may still be variable, but the plant owner is no longer subject to the price variations of the market.

Another example of a vertical acquisition would be an end manufacturer buying up the components of its supply chain to reduce uncertainty on timing of delivery. In the automobile industry, most components of an individual car are subcontracted out to smaller companies that provide the separate components to a major manufacturer like Ford or Volvo. Each of these subcontractors would be responsible for providing raw materials such as steel or glass, or a more sophisticated product like the radio, engine, or tires for the car. The main manufacturer will assemble the vehicle and put its own finishing touches on it, but many of the critical parts are built by third-party subcontractors.

In these situations, the main contractor, the car company, is reliant on the subcontractors for providing a quality product on time. If you bought a Ford with a radio that did not work, you would likely blame Ford and demand that they replace the radio rather than going to the subcontractor that made the radio. You really don't care who made the radio; you bought the car from Ford and want them to stand behind it.

Similarly, if you ordered a red Volkswagen Beetle to be delivered in time to give to your wife for Christmas, you want it ready by that time—no questions asked. You would not want to hear Volkswagen say the car was not ready, but it really was not their fault that a critical part was still missing.

A final form of vertical merger is when a company acquires one of its current distributors. Let's go back to the Ford example. Ford manufactures its own cars, but distributes them through a network of independent dealers nationwide. While Ford certainly manufactures a quality product, the local dealer completes the sale. If Ford were able to complete the car before Christmas, but the dealer was not open on Christmas Eve, we would still have a very unhappy customer. The acquisition of a dealer or distributer is another way that a company can more closely control the distribution of products to customers in a quality manner.

CONCLUSION

After all of these obvious issues, why do so many bad deals continue to happen? There is no simple answer to this in the complicated world of M&A. However, one thing we know for sure: The analysis and closing of a major international merger and acquisition is not as scientific and logical as many believe. It is often the softer issues around pressure to grow, personalities of the executives involved, and trying to take advantage of opportunistic situations that have as much influence on the process as the underlying economics of the transaction.

NOTES

1. IRR (internal rate of return) is a normal measure to determine the actual returns achieved on an acquisition. It takes the expected cash flows of the target company and discounts them back to the amount you have bid for the company. So deals with a higher IRR should be selected over lower IRR transactions. In theory, the projected IRR should be higher than the buyer's cost of capital to pay for the transaction. Otherwise, the buyer would be paying more for the company than merely keeping the cash and using it for other purposes.
2. Comment from James Eden, Dresdner Kleinwort Wasserstein, as quoted in the *Telegraph*: "Royal Bank of Scotland Investigation: The Full Story of How the World's Biggest Bank Went Bust," Harry Wilson, Philip Aldrick, and Kamal Ahmed, March 5, 2011.
3. Ibid.
4. Bank of America-Merrill Lynch, Harvard Business School, Case Study, June 7, 2010.
5. "J&J Synthes Takeover Obscuring Recalls in Makeover," *Real M&A*, Tara Lachapelle and Alex Nussbaum, April 19, 2011.
6. Michael Holland, chairman of Holland Company, New York.

CHAPTER 2

Buy or Build?

I love it when one bank buys another. They get the bank and I get all of the bank's customers!

—Vernon Hill, founder of Commerce Bank

A CASE STUDY: COMMERCE BANK

Way back in 1973, Vernon Hill came up with an idea for a new type of retail bank. Hill owned several Burger King restaurants. He understood what made a fast-food franchise successful and noticed a stark contrast between how a typical retail bank approached its customer versus how a fast-food restaurant approached the customer. Fast-food took a retail, customer-centric approach to business. Burger King was open late at night and over the weekend. You could enter any Burger King outlet, order your food, and be seated and eating within five minutes of entering the building. You knew that the quality of food at Burger King was consistent whether you were at a store in Pittsburgh, Pennsylvania, or in Moscow, Russia. You can enter a drive-through window at almost any hour of the day, never get out of your car, and be served a hamburger and fries within minutes. This is the essence of delighting the customer with your service.

Compare this retail, fast-food experience with what you find in a typical bank. Most banks close every day at 5 P.M. They are closed on weekends. Some of the bank's employees are not especially friendly or particularly concerned about the customer's experience once they walk through the doors. There are frequently long lines just to get to a teller. Many transactions can't be handled at the desk, and you are referred to another line where you have to wait further for a bank manager.

As just one example, have you ever tried to deposit loose change at your local bank? Over time, we all accumulate massive amounts of coins in jars, drawers, or simply sitting on the bedroom bureau. We have two choices. One is to spend the time to separate the quarters, dimes, nickels, and pennies and roll them into bank envelopes. Alternatively, some banks offer coin deposit machines that will count change automatically and directly deposit to your bank account. But they will normally charge you a 5 to 10 percent fee of the total amount deposited for the luxury of using their automated machines. The concept of a bank charging *me* to deposit *my* money into it has always seemed unfair to me. As a result, I have spent many late nights with my wife and kids separating quarters, dimes, nickels, and pennies into rolls of coins that the bank would allow me to deposit into its institution.

Hill wanted to build a different kind of bank. "The world," he reasoned, "did not need another 'me-too' bank." Hill's bank would be open until 8:00 at night, or even to midnight with a drive-through window in busier locations. He instituted a ten-minute rule stating that branches should open ten minutes early and stay open ten minutes late to overdeliver for their customers. Hill's strategy was simple, "I had no capital, no brand name, and I had to search for a way to differentiate from the other players."[1]

When customers came into Commerce Bank branches, they were met by a personable greeter who directed them to the appropriate area based on their needs. The branches were often magnificent two-story buildings in convenient locations that customers were proud to visit. Commerce Bank guaranteed that a potential customer could enter a branch unannounced and within 20 minutes leave with a savings account, a checking account, and a debit card allowing immediate access to any funds deposited in the bank. Hill's goal was to recreate the satisfying customer experience one finds at a fast-food restaurant in financial services; from the time customers entered the bank to the time they left, they were treated with warm, friendly service throughout.

With only $1.5 million of seed capital, Hill started a community bank in southern New Jersey that grew, without *any* acquisitions, into Pennsylvania, Delaware, and New York. Commerce Bank's deposit growth averaged over 30 percent per year. In 2001 alone, Commerce deposits grew by almost 40 percent while households served grew by 20 percent. By comparison, cumulative deposit growth in the United States was only 5 percent in 2001. Hill stated:

> *Other banks decided to push consumers out of the branch because it is the high-cost delivery channel. They wanted to push them online. We totally reject that. You can't name me one retailer in this country that has pushed people where they don't want to go and succeeded. But the banks decided to push to electronic delivery, and they have totally failed. Our model is, we are going to give you the best of every channel knowing you are going to use all of them. The result is not only do we have the highest deposit-rate growth in this country by a long factor, but our online usage is 34 percent, which is higher than Wells Fargo.*
>
> *I don't have to make a sale to you every day. Once you open your account I am making money on your balances. The big-bank attitude sees a customer as a cost, not a revenue generator. I don't see it that way.*
>
> *You cannot find me any retailer who has driven store count down and has survived, and yet banks think they can drive*

*customers out of their branches and still keep their business. I find
that very hard to understand. We have some branches that get
100,000 customer visits a month; the average branch gets 40,000.
As a comparison, an average McDonald's gets 25,000 per month.*[2]

Hill's view was that growing a business organically was infinitely more
efficient than growing via acquisition. He wanted to introduce a new brand
with a new culture, new building, new information systems, and a whole
different feel from the stodgy hundred-year-old banks he was competing
against. Hill stated,

*No one has built a power retailer in this country through mergers
and acquisitions. You can only build a delivery model like this from
scratch. Mergers and acquisitions are cost-cutting devices at their
heart, and the merger of cultures and the dilution of brand is a formula for failure. Every big bank merger in this country has failed.
It's easier to build a bank than to fix one.*[3]

In Chapter 5, we will discuss the difficulties in the structure, cultures,
personalities, and personal agendas involved in combining two companies.
Although difficult, they are manageable with the right techniques. However,
Hill's theory was, why introduce this uncertainty at all? Rather, let's hire
new employees and train them on the right way to do things from the
start. Why should we start with ancient IT systems that have been patched
together over continuous mergers of the target bank? Let's build our own,
clean IT system using today's technology. Let's make it a competitive
advantage for Commerce Bank rather than the distraction of trying to
combine old legacy systems.

Hill's business looked for cost efficiencies in other areas like IT systems,
suppliers, ATM contracts, and so on. However, rather than taking these
profits as income, Hill reinvested them into the business to improve the
overall customer experience, drive customer retention, and drive incremental revenue. The history of the ATM fee in New York City is a particularly
interesting story. Hill had built a terrific franchise throughout New Jersey,
Pennsylvania, and Delaware. However, he knew that he would need to
expand into New York to match up with the larger retail banks. Finding
office space in New York was not a problem. Finding select locations
for branches was not a problem. Finding employees was not a problem.
Expanding the customer service ethos that had worked so well in New
Jersey to the New York markets was not a problem.

But how would Commerce Bank be able to quickly install an ATM
network large enough to compete with the banks already established in

New York City? Customers were certainly going to demand easy access to Commerce Bank ATMs where they could transact business without having to pay a fee. Building a network of ATMs in New York was a very expensive proposition. Not only the cost of the machines themselves, but the cost of rental space for operations and servicing of machines would certainly eat up substantial levels of profit. To make matters worse, Commerce would need an extensive ATM network to provide the high level of service their customers were used to.

In Chapter 1 we used the comparison of building an Italian bank versus buying one. We concluded that buying a bank might be a more attractive proposition given the severe pressure on income and the pressure to enter a new market immediately. In this situation one temptation might be to purchase an established ATM network from a bank and pay a big premium for it given the immediacy of the need. However, no affordable ATM networks were for sale.

Hill then had a novel idea. Let's simply reimburse customers for out-of-network fees they have to pay to when using other banks' ATMs. Commerce could now provide the most extensive network of ATMs in New York City where *every bank's ATM* could be used by *any* Commerce customer at *any* time, free of charge. Commerce avoided the significant capital spend needed to build out an ATM network themselves. In addition, they wanted to enter New York now and not wait. What better way than to take existing installed ATMs rather than the time associated with building such a network machine by machine? In essence, Commerce was "renting" the entire network of New York City ATMs for a very reasonable fee.

Commerce branches were located on high-visibility street corners, had high cathedral ceilings, and were clean and serviced by friendly staff. You could go to any Commerce Bank in any of these states and they were essentially the same. "We know every screw in the model," Hill said. Most branches were built from scratch for about $1 million. With few exceptions, they had the same white-brick exterior capped with a black metal roof, the same black-and-white marble, the same no-frills checking and savings accounts, and the same lollipops and dog biscuits. "It makes life easier for customers," says chief marketing officer John Cunningham. "They know what the deal is wherever they visit one of our banks."

Location of bank branches was critical. High-traffic areas were sought oftentimes within yards of subway stops or bus stops. Hill approved the location of each branch personally to ensure consistency and ultimate visibility for his product. A new branch was frequently next to an established competitor, but that did not scare Hill off. In fact, each Commerce branch was awarded $5,000 if a nearby branch closed, failing to be able to compete with Commerce Bank. The formula continued to work as Commerce opened branch after branch after branch. Commerce's branches became profitable within 18 months in an industry where an average bank took three years to break even.

Commerce Bank retained a strong focus on customer service, attempting not only to meet customer needs, but to exceed them on a consistent basis. For example, if it rained, Commerce employees guided customers back to their car under a Commerce umbrella. Each branch had not only candies for the kids, but biscuits for the dogs! A greeter met each person as they entered the branch. Hill stated:

> *Commerce Bank had an internal program called WOW to train customers in the way of doing business at the bank. WOW was an integral part of the training process at Commerce University, a full-time education and training facility staffed by 41 employees. All new employees underwent an intense introduction to Commerce culture during a class called "Traditions," characterized as "part game show, part training session, and part common sense." The course was designed to be enjoyable while providing new employees with the best ways to delight bank customers.*[4]

Proper staffing was a critical part of the Commerce recipe for success. In a traditional acquisition, employees are brought on with preexisting culture preferences and biases. By hiring new employees, Commerce was able to train them from the start with the right values and approach. This required a very selective approach to find the unique type of person who would thrive in this environment. For example, over 2,000 interviews were conducted to hire 40 people in New York. However, when they found the right talent and trained them properly, employees were here to stay. As they gained more experience, they became more adept at oversatisfying customers time and time again.

Hill not only discouraged M&A as a means of growth, he used the M&A activity of others as a competitive advantage by adding employees and customers shed from the merged banks. Employees can become frustrated after going through normal acquisitions. They are asked to learn different systems and a different culture and to get comfortable with different pay packages and benefits. A new bank with a new concept several blocks down the street might seem particularly appealing to the alternative of staying where you are and having new rules imposed on you. Why go through an exhausting integration process when there is a hot new bank down the street with enthusiastic employees and an exciting new culture?

Similarly, many consumers had become quite frustrated with the constant consolidation of banking institutions in the United States. Each time their bank got acquired, they received a new checking and savings account number. Each time, the form of the statement, terms offered, bank hours, and so on changed to the acquirer's bank format. A new bank card with a new account number was required every time. Commerce sold against this. They were the homegrown bank that would not acquire or be acquired. Customers could count on the first-rate, consistent service they had become accustomed to at Commerce.

With some of its competitors offering better rates, Commerce had to ensure that its value proposition was clear in customers' minds. Commerce deliberately competed on service, not price. It paid lower rates on deposits in order to pay for enhanced service. The question was, how far should Commerce take differentiating on service? How would this high service model translate among different cultures? Would all customers react positively to this attention? Perhaps some wanted to just get in and out without speaking to anyone. Many of these questions would be answered by Hill's next project, attempting to bring a customer-centric banking model to the U.K.

A CASE STUDY: METRO BANK

Hill's latest creation is a similar concept directed toward consumers in the United Kingdom called Metro Bank. Metro Bank was the first bank to receive a new banking license from the U.K. Financial Services Authority in over 100 years. Metro Bank has expanded quickly since opening its first branch in 2010. It has raised £6.6 billion ($8.5 billion) in customer deposits, has over 40 stores, and is now one of the top 250 largest public companies in the entire United Kingdom. Each of the store locations are in high-traffic areas, normally within one-half mile of a tube station. The heavy foot traffic and inviting branch facilities are drivers to high customer growth and retention.

I had the opportunity to visit a new Metro branch opening near my home in Kensington, United Kingdom. The grand opening included balloons, free gifts, face painting, "Metro Man," and even biscuits for your dog. It was quite the party with lines of patrons waiting to get into the bank. Hill and his executive team were present to greet customers and answer questions.

The event lasted from Friday morning through Sunday night. By Sunday night the crowds had finally started to subside. My daughter and I happened to be passing by the branch on the way to a Sunday dinner along Kensington High Street. The bank was quieter now as people prepared to go back to work on Monday. But there was Hill at the front door *still* greeting visitors after a very long weekend. Now *that* is customer service. Here is a man with substantial wealth willing to spend his entire weekend opening up a new bank branch far away from home.

Metro Bank follows similar principles to Commerce Bank in the United States. Late-night hours, grand bank branches, and welcoming staff are all standard procedure. Using newer technology, Metro Bank promises that within 20 minutes of entry, customers can leave with a new checking account, a new savings account, *and* the bank card used to process ATM transactions. Metro guarantees that a live person will answer the phone within two rings when you call customer service, which is very different from the endless recording loops you end up in when calling your traditional bank. Metro views customer service as a profit center, not a cost center. By delighting customers with great service, Metro will generate incremental revenue that more than offsets the incremental cost it takes to provide it.

Now, imagine how difficult it would be to drive that philosophy with a decade-old U.K. bank. Hill said, "If I could make Commerce Bank work in the U.S., it should be easy in the U.K. given the lousy service that the banks provide here." Hill was convinced that he could outperform the competition. However, Metro's approach can only work with a unique culture around its management and staff. The main principles of this culture at Metro include:

- Create a culture to match your model.
- Culture must be very clear and very pervasive: "Buy in or opt out."
- Hire for attitude and train for skills.
- Over-train.
- Over-reinforce.
- Make everyone an owner.[5]

Changing the culture of an acquired company is extremely difficult. Established norms and biases can embed a strong culture in an organization that is very hard to change. One of the largest risks to successful M&A is a clash of cultures between buyer and seller. By building a business from scratch, Hill could recruit people who had the values and train them to the unique culture of the bank rather than trying to retrain them from their old habits and ways of doing business.

The Metro Model includes the following fundamentals:

- Core customer deposits create value:
  - Access to low-cost customer deposits is hugely valuable in the difficult capital markets of today.

- Customers will live with lower rates for a better retail experience:
  - I often ask my MBA students how many of them know what their savings deposit account pays them within 25 basis points. Although there are normally several students who have it pegged to the basis point, the majority of my students have no idea what interest rate they get on deposits. Hill's view is that rates on deposit are an *inelastic* component of banking consumer demand (i.e., the rate on deposits does not drive the decision making of most people on where to deposit their money).
  - On the other hand, a quality banking experience is quite elastic (i.e., customers really care about service). Customers will make their banking decisions based on the quality of customer service, nice branches, and efficient operations. This drives better loyalty and retention of accounts.
- Great business creates fans, not just customers:
  - By overdelivering to customers, they can be your best advertising in the market. Happy customers will continue to use your bank. Fans will promote your bank to friends and family, driving new accounts. This is the best form of advertising Metro could ask for.

In the first chapter, we used the example of a buying versus building an Italian bank. In that case, we determined that, if properly done, an outright purchase may be the best way forward. So why are we recommending this build strategy of Hill's now? The pros from such a model are:

- *Build you own culture.* In a build, you get to introduce your culture and strategy to people before they have become contaminated by existing norms and biases. People can be focused on the right ways to do things versus being constrained by bad practices.
- *No premium is awarded.* In most major M&A, significant premiums must be paid to induce a seller to sell. Building a business yourself does not require payment of a premium; you get the assets you want and the people you hire for cost.
- *Better control.* With proper management, a build scenario can be closely monitored by senior management. Progress can be monitored on a daily basis against stated criteria. Alternatively, the complexity of large-scale acquisitions requires immediate integration, often without adequate attention to detail.
- *Better management of capital.* Rather than paying a large amount up front, builds can be over time as funds become more readily available. Projects can be accelerated if the funds end up being available earlier than expected.

- *Hand-select a good team.* It is very difficult to evaluate a senior management team, regardless of the amount of time you have for due diligence. People are very rarely who/what you believe them to be, particularly after only two days of due diligence. In build scenarios, you can take the time to get to know your employees, with no time pressure on reaching a conclusion.

There are significant cons to this model of combination as well, including:

- *Time.* An acquisition provides immediate access to the company, the market, and the financial results. Despite how well organized, a build scenario will take significantly longer time. Hiring people, obtaining appropriate licenses, finding premises, and so on all delay the start-up of the operation where a buy scenario provides immediate access.
- *Local geography and product knowledge.* In a build scenario the senior management team may not have a good awareness of the country of entry or the product being developed. This makes it more difficult to quickly grow the business and execute on the opportunity. Hiring product and geography expertise can help. However, there will still be a learning curve in most build scenarios that is not present in a buy situation.

IS THERE ANYTHING IN BETWEEN?

We have now seen examples of (1) buys that work, (2) buys that don't work, (3) builds that work, and (4) builds that don't work. To further complicate matters, there is a final strategy that fits in the middle of these two—the partnership or joint venture (JV). Joint ventures are often used as a bridge between a formal purchase and a new build.

In a typical JV, two firms agree to partner to form a third independent company to address a particular market, geography, or industry. Depending on the structure, 100 percent of each party's existing business could be contributed, a piece of their existing business could be contributed, or it could be a completely new area that the two firms want to address via a JV structure.

However, JV structures can have issues as well, including the following:

- *Misalignment of interests.* While many parties to JVs start with the best intentions, it is easy to get off course as the JV progresses. Some JVs perform poorly due to cultural differences or miscommunications at the start of the process. Priorities can change over time as the situation of each JV partner changes. Having a clear understanding up front of the purpose of the JV, the ultimate goal, and the time period to continue the venture can be critical to success. However, no one can predict what will happen to the two JV partners after the partnership documents are signed that could change the situation.

- *Who is in charge?* Many JVs are structured as 50/50 partnerships between the parties to the JV. This is done to align the interests and make sure that each partner adds enough economic value in the JV to justify their attention. However, this absolute sharing of power can make it difficult to reach critical decisions quickly, particularly if the two parties to the JV don't agree on an important issue. Because no one party is in control, the decision-making process can be slow.

  Some JVs are split as 49 percent ownership for one party and 51 percent to the other. One party who is in control can help mitigate some of the decision-making issues. However, even then, both parties will want the ability to have control over major decisions such as large investments, markets to enter, or decisions around the ultimate dissolution of the JV.

- *Liability.* As we will see in the Dow Corning JV case study later in this chapter, each party to the agreement can be held jointly and severally liable for the activities of the partnership. In other words, you as one party to the JV can be liable for what your JV partner does even if you were not involved or did not know about it. This makes it very critical to be comfortable with any partner you decide to JV with.

- *Ending the JV.* Unless specifically stated otherwise, JVs are set up to continue in perpetuity. This makes it very difficult to dissolve a JV if and when the time is right. The two parties may have very differing views on the value of the JV and its prospects for the future. This can cause a bit of a messy "divorce" unless formal dissolution principles were established at the start of the JV.

- *Management distraction.* In JVs that are less than 100 percent of the respective parent companies, each partner to the JV has a core business to run. Entrance into a new market or geography via JV can distract each of the parties from growing their existing business.

On the other hand, structured properly, JVs can add substantial value to each party, including:

- *Flexibility.* JVs can provide operating flexibility if structured right. They are essentially partnerships between two existing entities. Each party to the JV can agree to whatever they want the purpose of the JV to be, its operating structure, and its ultimate performance target. This can be done outside of the core businesses of the JV partners to limit, but not eliminate, the amount of distraction to the management while exploring new markets via the JV entity.

- *Limited liability.* In theory, the JV structure limits the amount of liability to the equity that each party has contributed to the JV. In other words, liabilities incurred by the JV will only pertain up to the value of the existing equity in the JV. The equity of the parties to the JV is legally separated and cannot be used to satisfy the liabilities of the JV. However, as we will see in Dow Corning, in egregious cases the courts have "pierced the corporate veil" and sought damages directly from the parents to the JV even though the legal documents indicate a separation.

- *Synergies.* In a classic JV, each party contributes something different to the entity. In some cases this may be as simple as one party providing capital to another entity that has a great concept to grow, but not enough capital to implement it. In other cases, it is a combination of two unique technologies that drives the JV structure. Finally, many JVs are done to help one partner expand into the geography of another partner. This often happens in emerging markets where a partner with a good product or technology aligns with another partner who is in the country and understands local laws and regulations.

In any case, combining the best qualities of two parties is the underlying rationale for most JV combinations. However, if not structured properly or set up for the wrong purpose, JVs can have a very negative effect on the partners who signed the agreement.

A CASE STUDY: DOW CORNING JOINT VENTURE

One example of a JV not going well is the breast implant controversy surrounding Dow Corp.'s JV with Corning Inc. Dow Corning had developed a silicone grease used to prevent moisture issues in aircraft engines when they reached a certain altitude. A joint venture was established in 1943 to investigate other uses for this newly developed silicone product. The venture worked extremely well for decades as silicone was used to solve a multitude of other problems it was not originally designed for.

That was up until the idea to use silicone for breast implants in women. Throughout the 1980s and 1990s, class-action lawsuits claimed that Dow Corning's silicone breast implants caused systemic health problems. The breast implants could deteriorate and leak, wreaking havoc upon a woman's immune system. The claims first centered on breast cancer and then migrated to a range of autoimmune diseases, including lupus, rheumatoid arthritis, and various neurological problems. This led to numerous lawsuits beginning in 1984 and culminating in a large class action settlement several years later. As a result, Dow Corning was put into bankruptcy protection for nine years, ending in June 2004.

To make matters worse, the plaintiffs decided to go further than the equity in the Dow Corning joint venture, to "pierce the corporate veil" and go after the parent companies, Dow and Corning Inc. As discussed earlier, JVs are normally set up to guard the parent companies from just this sort of claim. The argument states that a JV is a separate legal entity where the parent companies are investors in the entity, but not responsible for areas outside of its net worth. Therefore, damages can only be sought from the JV itself, not the parents.

However, due to the egregious nature of the claims in this case, the courts held Dow and Coring liable even outside of their JV. They were each sued directly for damages of the suit. Hoping to put the long and tortuous breast implant litigation process behind it, Dow and Corning agreed to pay $2.4 billion to settle the more than 300,000 claims against it.

A CASE STUDY: BUCKNELL INDUSTRIES

A final example of a failed JV was a technology company that had developed best-in-class technology around computer simulation—let's call it Bucknell Industries. More specifically, they had applied this technology to the trucking industry and created a truck driving experience that simulated the actual driving of a tractor trailer truck within 99 percent of the actual experience of driving and without ever having to hit the road to get it.

Users sat in an actual truck cab manufactured to the exact specifications of trucks on the road at that time. The cab was set on a platform supported by several pistons and surrounded by video screens. When you sat inside the cab, you felt like you were driving in real life.

The video screens had several settings that allowed for different driving environments. If you went over a bump, you felt the bump in the cab. You could press a button and it would start to snow on the video screens. At the same time, your breaks would slip a bit as you tried to stop on the snow. When you went around a turn, the truck bed leaned to the side to create the feeling of an actual driving experience.

The main purpose of the simulator was to provide the practice necessary to obtain a commercial driver's license (CDL) in the United States.

Although time in the simulator did not count toward CDL, this training made the student much better prepared for the on-the-road portion of the CDL exam. Another goal was to improve the driving efficiency of students. The gear components on the simulator cab mimicked the actual components of a truck. A computer program tracked the student's efficiency in switching gears during the driving process. Studies showed that the simulator helped improve fuel efficiency by as much as 20 percent for those who trained in these simulators.

Safety was the main concern for customers deciding to use this technology. An increased awareness around corporate social responsibility and the massive expense from lost time due to accidents resulted in the creation of a Safety Officer at many large corporations. This person's role was to develop better safety procedures for the organization and to reduce the cost associated with downtime for accidents. There was a natural draw for safety officers toward anything that could reduce accidents and increase efficiency. Bucknell's technology was a wonderful solution to these needs.

Bucknell took its simulator training to the next step. They developed a second product, a replica of a police cruiser surrounded by screens to create a virtual driving experience. Bucknell could put two police cruisers next to each other, connect the computers and simulate a high-speed chase in very safe conditions. This was incredibly powerful as training because a high-speed chase on the open roads was simply not practical.

Bucknell's product could be marketed to all of the state and local police departments as a way to increase productivity and safety in a no-risk environment. In fact, the company had several testimonials from municipal police departments that had trained on Bucknell simulators and saw the benefits in reduced accidents, as more police officers in the United States get killed by car accidents than they do by bullets each year.

At the time of the JV, Bucknell had a third product in development, an airport tug simulator. Airport tugs are the machines that push an airplane to and from the gate on departure and arrival. Think about that for a minute. What do you need to train a tug operator? For 100 percent of the experience you would need a spare tug, a spare airplane, and a spare inactive runway to practice on! Think about the massive idle equipment and cost involved in such a training exercise. By using a simulator, Bucknell could recreate 99 percent of this experience in a private setting without the safety concerns of training on an active runway.

Bucknell had spent many painstaking years developing this product. They had invested significant research and development capital and were now ready to commercialize its operation. However, as a family-run business, they did not have adequate capital to get the business to the next level. This is a classic reason for a joint venture, where one party has access to technology and another has access to capital. This can be a very powerful combination when the technology is a good one and the partners can work together effectively.

In this case, a second company, let's call it GINT, provided the capital. However, capital alone was not enough to get this project off the ground. GINT ran into a variety of issues in attempting to execute on this JV. First of all, they could not decide whether they were building simulators to sell the units themselves or to keep the units and train people on them. Bucknell Industries had historically used the units exclusively for sale. This was a relatively straightforward approach. Building the simulators had become routine. There was an adequate order backlog to continue selling units as they were made with nice profit margins.

However, the JV decided to manufacture its own units to train customers. While this seems like a simple change, there are many complications to it. For example, if you were going to train, you needed training course materials. So, a whole curriculum around the simulator needed to be developed from scratch. The second thing was setting up training facilities to house the machines and bring students for the course. GINT soon realized that being in the real estate business was much different than being in the simulator manufacturing business. There were also several cultural issues that emerged after GINT and Bucknell had agreed to partner up.

After a long and difficult journey, Bucknell Industries and GINT decided to part ways. The philosophies on how to grow the business had not been set clearly and agreed to up front. The ideas around execution varied significantly. GINT also underestimated the amount of capital that would be required to build out training stations across the country, provide local trainers, and develop the curriculum.

To make matters worse, GINT had not included pre-agreed dissolution policies in the agreement. When both parties decided to terminate the JV, there was no roadmap around how the assets would be split, what would happen to management teams, what to do with remaining capital, who owned the Bucknell brand name, and so on. This further complicated the divorce and distracted each company's management team from their day-to-day activities on their core businesses.

CONCLUSION

We probably have you totally confused by now. Do I buy? Do I build? Do I JV? Or do I just do nothing? The simple answer is that it depends.

Each one of these combinations can be effective if structured properly. The keys are to:

- *Know the party you are working with.* Whether it is an outright purchase, a JV, or a start-up, knowing the people you are working with is critical to success. In JVs or start-ups you need to have a feel for the culture and how well the employees will work with you regardless of structure. Picking the right management team is the single largest determinant of success in any business combination.

  This is even more difficult in a 100 percent acquisition. Oftentimes access to management is limited by the due diligence process. You need to try to get a feel for the people, their biases, and their culture as compared to the characteristics of your current company.

- *Be clear on objectives.* Having a clear set of objectives up front that both parties agree to is critical, particularly in a joint venture arrangement. In a start-up, employees coming in need to know what the purpose of the business is, its long-term goals, and what they are being asked to contribute to achieve them.

  In a 100 percent sale, communication at the start is critical. Employees will be anxious about being acquired. They will want to know what is going to happen to them and their colleagues and how they will be treated by the new regime. Having clear, direct, and concise discussions up front can get the diligence process started on a positive note.

- *Clearly define exit options.* Despite the best intentions, many deals will go bad. In a JV context, having agreed dissolution procedures can vastly simplify the exit process. In a start-up, employees should know what is expected of them and also know what will happen if the combination does not work. Other tools include retention bonuses, termination clauses, and so on that can help align the interests of the target company employees with those of the buyer.

- *Understand the culture.* Ensuring the right culture is critical to the success of *any* business combination, but JVs in particular. As we saw with Bucknell Industries, having an alignment of cultures and priorities is important to success. And as we will see in Chapter 5 with AOL Time Warner, a misalignment of cultures can ruin any venture no matter how much sense they seem to make at the start.

- *Have patience.* Patience is just as critical for any business combination. Any combination invariably takes longer than the parties expect regardless of the form of combination. Particularly in start-up situations, it may take 9 to 12 months to even see if the business proposition makes sense, never mind implementing it and driving revenue from it. In a JV context, you must maintain patience with your partner. Cultural differences can be quite significant, particularly in cross-border JVs. Having the patience to get to know your partner and to be cooperative are critical to success.

- *Pay attention.* Whether it is a 100 percent acquisition, a JV, or a start-up, you simply cannot underestimate the amount of effort that will be required to make it work. Adequate management attention is critical to any deal working. JVs, start-ups, and purchases are major initiatives that will stretch a firm. The rewards can be immense. However, no business combination will be successful without adequate attention from employees, supervisors, and most importantly, senior management. Senior management must set the tone and example about how critical these combinations are to transforming your business.

The ups and downs of the global economy over the past several years have put a lot of pressure on leaders at all levels. Getting good business done is not easy. Business combinations can be a clever way to stimulate growth in areas where your core markets are suffering. The form of combination is actually not that important. The same principles apply whether it is a start-up, a JV, or a 100 percent acquisition. Having the vision, the stamina, and the cultural sensitivity to make it work will determine whether you are successful. Business combinations are a big risk that many people fail to fully appreciate. However, done right they can jump-start your company and your career.

NOTES

1. Commerce Bank, Harvard Case Study, October 3, 2006.
2. Ibid.
3. Ibid.
4. Ibid.
5. Metro Bank Company presentation, September 2010.

CHAPTER 3

Let the Buyer Beware

What is Bad? All that proceeds from weakness.
                                                    —Friedrich Nietzsche

Due diligence is the investigation that the buyer completes on the target company to determine whether to buy, any potential issues, and how much to pay. For example, assume that you are in the market for a new house. You would want to review the seller's disclosure list of any problems, inspect the property, see if there are any liens on the title to the house, arrange a mortgage, and so on. It is no different in buying a company. You need to make sure you know what you are buying *before* you legally commit to purchase it. However, while this sounds like simple common sense to most, there are numerous cases where sophisticated buyers have not done adequate due diligence in multibillion-dollar acquisitions. And the results can be a disaster.

In fact, one of the most common problems in all M&A transactions is a buyer's failure to complete an adequate amount of due diligence. Take the case of Bank of America buying Merrill Lynch for $50 billion. Bank of America decided to purchase Merrill Lynch between a Friday night and a Monday morning.[1] How does anyone complete an entire diligence process on a global, massively complex bank in the span of 48 hours? Most people take more time deciding whether to buy a new home or car than Bank of America took to commit to a multibillion-dollar deal. Was it that management truly understood what they were buying and were fully ready to move forward, or were there other reasons like pressure from the government to close?

As Charles Duhigg of the *New York Times* stated at the time, "In 48 hours you can't do due diligence. You can't really take a bank's books and determine where the liabilities are, where the risks are, who's been hiding what to try and get a good bonus this year. It's impossible to know within 48 hours what you are actually buying."[2] The people involved in the transaction were pushed to close by Sunday evening, but knew there was a problem right away. John Thain, CEO of Merrill Lynch, stated, "Hank (Paulson) in particular was very strongly encouraging me to get the deal done."[3] Avoiding the pressures to close quickly, regardless of the source of this pressure, and having the discipline to truly understand what you are buying before you commit are key aspects to a successful transaction.

WACHOVIA BUYS GOLDEN WEST

In a second example, Wachovia Corporation decided to enter the (at the time) lucrative subprime mortgage market in California. They saw an opportunity to expand assets and generate high-margin business. In hindsight, Wachovia purchased at the exact wrong part of the economic cycle, right before the housing bubble burst. One could argue whether there were clear signs of the bubble prior to Wachovia's commitment to purchase. But a more thorough and detailed due diligence process would have at least uncovered some of the issues specific to Golden West and influenced Wachovia to either lower its price or abandon the acquisition altogether.

To provide some context to the deal, Wachovia Corporation was formed by the merger of Charlotte, NC–based First Union Corporation and Winston-Salem–based Wachovia Corporation in 2001. Wachovia provided a broad range of banking, wealth management, asset management, capital management, and corporate and investment banking products and services. It was the fourth largest banking company and the third largest retail brokerage firm in the United States. Golden West Financial was the second largest savings and loan bank in the United States. It operated branches under the name of World Savings Bank. Golden West also owned Atlas Advisers, an investment advisor to the Atlas family of mutual funds and annuities. So a combination of these two large, but diverse businesses did make some strategic sense at a high level.

Golden West took pride in its "high-return, risk-averse" strategy for growth. It was also well renowned for its sound and robust underwriting policy targeting creditworthy borrowers with high-quality mortgages that were secured by conservatively appraised, reasonably priced residential properties. In 2005, Golden West's lending team originated a record mortgage volume of $51.5 billion, 99 percent of which were adjustable-rate mortgages. At December 31, 2005, Golden West's total assets stood at $125 billion. Herbert and Marion Sandler, founders of Golden West, owned around 10 percent of the shares in 2005. In 2006, *Fortune* magazine named Golden West Financial the "Most Admired Company" in the mortgage services business.

Wachovia was faced with the same questions many large corporations encounter regarding shareholder pressure to keep growing. They had to decide whether to enter into the mortgage market in California by building a presence themselves (referred to as "de-novo") or by buying someone who already had material market share. Wachovia did not want to miss out on the frenetic pace of the mortgage business that had emerged in California, so they went with the faster option, paying up to buy it. While this provided an immediate presence to a new market, it also opened up Wachovia to potential latent legal, tax, risk, or other liabilities that were not apparent on the date they closed.

On May 7, 2006, Wachovia announced the acquisition of Golden West. The deal valued Golden West at 2.8× book value and added $125 billion of assets to Wachovia's balance sheet. Most of these assets were home mortgages with a heavy concentration in California. The deal enhanced Wachovia's footprint in California, increased its retail distribution, and gave Wachovia significant exposure to mortgage loans and an immediate position among the top five banks in the Western United States.

An opportunity to grow assets by 20 percent with an acquisition in the hottest housing segment, California, was too lucrative to pass up. Perceived synergies around shared distribution channels, cross-selling of products, and strong future growth prospects were just some of the factors that drove Wachovia toward this acquisition. Wachovia CEO Ken Thompson stated, "For four decades, Golden West has taken industrywide challenges in stride and maintained a singular focus as a risk-averse residential mortgage portfolio lender. The result is virtually no credit losses even in the toughest year in its history."

For Golden West, the intention to sell was largely driven by the desire of the CEO and the company's 10 percent stakeholders, Herbert and Marion Sandler, to retire after building Golden West into a major bank. The Sandlers had recorded close to 20 percent annual earnings growth for most of the previous four decades. Fortunately for the Golden West shareholders, their timing was impeccable as the sale happened at the peak of the housing boom. Had they not sold at or around this time, Golden West would have incurred the massive losses that were ultimately taken on by the buyer.

Most of the analysts tracking Wachovia approved of the deal at the time but mentioned several risks, including:

- A slowdown in new mortgage acquisitions in Golden West in 2006 vs. 2005.
- Integration risks associated with the deal.
- An equity market downturn that could affect Wachovia's brokerage and investment banking income.

Analysts liked the potential for cross-selling through Golden West's extensive branch network, its low level of underperforming assets, and the positive risk profile of Golden West's business.

However, there were questions around why Wachovia would take such a big exposure to the California mortgage market at a time it was thought to be overvalued. Complicating this was the fact that Wachovia completed only *one week* of due diligence prior to committing to this purchase. The high premium paid for the bank was questioned. Analysts also pointed to the significant execution risk involved in converting a thrift franchise like Golden West with only two products to a full service bank like Wachovia with multiple product lines and a cross-selling of products among these lines.

But even though the stock analysts in general supported the deal, Wachovia investors reacted negatively to the announcement, with the stock price declining by 7 percent on a single day. The stock continued to under-perform the S&P 500 financial index over the next month. As one analyst stated, "I think the stock is down because investors want this company to focus on internal growth and its management prefers to continue building through acquisitions. Management is either not getting the message or disagrees with it."[4]

Golden West continued to add mortgages at a fast pace to meet the aggressive targets put into the acquisition forecasts. In most mergers, the buyer's personnel will take control of the deal immediately after closing to drive post-deal strategy and to implement their policies and procedures. In this case, however, executives from Golden West took control of all areas of mortgage lending and they continued to follow Golden West's more aggressive form of underwriting loans. This decision ultimately exposed the combined company to material losses.

One example of Golden West products was a "Quick Qualifier" program where the applicant's employment, income, and assets were approved with minimal or no verification on the part of Golden West. Also referred to as "liar loans," the bank would trust whatever the customer wrote on the application about his ability to repay without checking any independent sources to verify the data. Instead of auditing the customer's credit history, Golden West focused on getting accurate appraisals on the home being mortgaged to ensure that the value of the home exceeded the amount of the mortgage. The theory was that if the borrower ever defaulted on the mortgage, the bank could repossess the house, sell it, and pay off the mortgage with these proceeds. Banks rationalized that housing prices would always continue to rise as they had in the past years and there would never be any losses as long as they did not lend more than the house was worth.

But even this was not good enough. A new product was introduced called "pick a payment" loan where the homeowner decided how much she could afford to pay each month. If the homeowner could not afford to make a monthly payment, she could simply add any unpaid amount to the mort-gage principle balance and pay it later. In other words, rather than having to pay down the loan balance each month, the loan amount could actually be increased at the option of the buyer if she did not have the cash to make payment. This strategy could theoretically work, but only if housing prices continued to go up in pace with the mortgage increases. When the housing bubble burst and prices suddenly dropped, these pick-a-payment loans had an even bigger shortage between the amount due and the underlying value of the loan.

Golden West's aggressive lending practices continued at a fast pace, even as the housing market was starting to crash. In the good years, Golden West's robust portfolio performance was helped by rising home prices, rather than by sound underwriting of the customers taking out these mortgages. It was hard to actually lose money when the values of homes continued to escalate each year. However, as incidents of default increased and the housing market values plunged, banks were caught with loans where they had lent more than the value of the home (i.e., the loans were underwater). As a result, losses started to mount quickly.

So what went wrong? Why would Wachovia get into an overheated California mortgage market via acquisition at exactly the wrong time? Shouldn't they have seen these problems coming? This sequence of events highlights the importance of a thorough independent analysis of the risks and rewards of a potential acquisition. Wachovia completed only one week of due diligence before agreeing to buy Golden West. This is not nearly enough time to understand a complicated bank like Golden West, not to mention the ability to adequately assess a multibillion-dollar mortgage portfolio at the top of the housing market.

Each M&A transaction requires a different set of due diligence skills to be effective. For example, the consulting firm you choose to help analyze an oil and gas company might be quite different from what you need for a financial services company. The skillset, understanding of the industry, and sensitivity to deal-specific issues can take on a very different profile. Some consultants are better at evaluating big-picture issues like macroeconomic trends and industry strategies. Others are more pragmatic and help deal with integration planning and micro-level-deal economics. Picking the right consultant, one you can trust for the task at hand, can be important.

As we will see later in this book, international deals complicate due diligence even further. An analysis of companies in Western economies is very different than emerging markets. A different set of consultants can be required depending on the region to understand local laws and regulations, tax codes, and human resource issues. Most deals today are complex global acquisitions that require all of these various skillsets for the same transaction. Not having local people available in each country where the target does business can be a critical mistake.

There are ten best practices that can improve the due diligence process and help buyers avoid the mistakes seen time after time in major acquisitions:

1. *Establish one centralized person who is responsible for all aspects of due diligence.* This central point of control can be helpful to coordinate the outside providers, mobilize the internal resources of the buyer,

and ensure that adequate attention gets paid to the multiple issues that will invariably arise. This one point of contact can also provide consistent and reliable feedback to the CEO and board to make an informed decision on whether to proceed with the transaction.

2. *Avoid the temptation to be forced into a deal before you have completed adequate due diligence.* While this sounds simple, it is often overlooked in major deals. It is hard to know what truly happened behind closed doors in BofA's purchase of Merrill. However, the evidence indicates that there was at least some level of government pressure on Merrill CEO John Thain and BofA CEO Ken Lewis to close the deal by Sunday night to avert a failure of Merrill by Monday morning. This put these CEOs in a very difficult position, trying to balance the interests of their shareholders with the impact any failure of Merrill would have on the global economy.

3. *Hire experts, but check their work!* Too often, buyers hand over complete control and accountability for due diligence to outside accountants, lawyers, consultants, and so forth. While these parties are necessary and helpful, ultimate accountability for each deal lies with the person "cutting the check" (i.e., the buyer). The information provided by all outside consultants needs to be closely reviewed and independently evaluated. It is also important to look at this information in totality to get a perspective on the deal overall. Legal risks, tax issues, overall strategy, and so on often interact and influence each other. They should be evaluated at a high level to determine the overall risks and rewards of the deal.

4. *Try to maintain objectivity.* After spending weeks or months on due diligence, it is easy for a deal team to lose their perspective. But in some cases, the best deals are the ones that are avoided. Teams can't get emotionally attached to a deal, regardless of how long they have been looking at it. One best practice seen in private equity is to introduce a completely new deal team shortly before the transaction comes up for final approval. This allows for a fresh perspective from people not as emotionally involved in the transaction and often uncovers issues that may have been missed.

5. *Have an integration professional involved from Day 1 of the due diligence.* All too often the person running the due diligence disappears after the deal is signed and hands it off to a new integration team who have little context around the deal. Having an integration person involved from the start of the diligence allows her to understand the issues, get to know the management team, and have an understanding of the strategy. One best practice is to have a "100-Day Plan" agreed to

before the documents are signed so that on the first day after closing the integration team can hit the ground running to implement the buyer's strategy. The first several weeks after the deal closes can be the most critical of all due to the uncertainty of employees and the risk of proper handoffs during the ownership transition.

6. *Establish a formal transition services agreement between buyer and seller.* This provides for the seller to continue performing such necessary services as payroll, tax preparation, IT, and so on until the buyer has the time to move these processes to their people and systems. However, there is often tension between the seller, who wants to move on as soon as possible, and the buyer, who may want more time to convert to new systems. Most transition services agreements end up being three to six months in duration.

7. *Check up on acquisition promises.* Too often a deal team is allowed to make overly aggressive assumptions in an acquisition to justify a price to win the deal, but *never* gets subsequently challenged as to how these plans turned out. Better control can be set around acquisition approvals by establishing a process and an expectation that the forecasts presented to the board will be periodically reviewed and compared to actual results. People act differently when they know they will be held accountable for results.

8. *Culture* is such an important factor that we have a separate chapter dedicated to it. In a due diligence context it is critical to understand the differences in the laws, customs, and regulatory framework when doing international deals. Your diligence team needs to include either in-house resources, external consultants, or both who have experience and appreciation for how things are different, both pre-close in terms of enforcing your purchase contract and post-close in the risks of running the business.

9. *Remember the people!* Of all the best practices defined here, this is one of the most important. The quality of the target company management team can fundamentally determine whether a deal is successful. These are the people guiding your investment and stewarding the (at times) billions of dollars spent to purchase the target. But a formal assessment of the management team is frequently overlooked. Deal teams spend significant time with lawyers to understand potential liability, with consultants to map out a strategy, and with accountants to understand the numbers. But the decision on management is often made after a few meetings or even a two-hour dinner! More and more buyers are starting to professionalize this evaluation with psychometric testing, personality profiling, and an analysis of how the management team interacts as a

group. This last point is particularly important if the new company is to be run by a combination of the management team of the buyer and the seller.

10. *Be especially careful around revenue synergies.* As discussed earlier, the concept is that incremental value can be created by combining the best qualities of the buyer and the seller. There are two basic forms of synergies, cost and revenue.

   Cost synergies are not always easy to deliver, but are generally fairly controllable by the buyer. All of the actions required to generate these synergies are within management's control. Buyers can easily close stores, reduce work forces, and deliver the value assumed in their projections for the acquisition.

   Revenue synergies are more complex and harder to deliver. They involve things like a combination of the company's customer bases, distribution channels, or product offerings. A classic example of such synergies is when a big pharmaceutical company buys a small-to-medium-size biotech firm for access to a new drug. Pharma companies need a pipeline of drugs to replace those that are aging or becoming obsolete, or where their patent protection is about to expire.

   Rather than spend the research and development to constantly invest in new drugs, pharma companies will buy drugs already approved from smaller, more flexible biotech firms that are arguably better at innovation and creating new things. Classic revenue synergies can be created by introducing these drugs into the well-established distribution channels and customer bases of the pharma companies. Few incremental sales or marketing efforts are required as the customer relationships are already mature. But as we have seen time and time again, revenue synergies are much harder to control and deliver. One of the best examples of planned synergies that never materialized was AOL's acquisition of Time Warner.

AOL TIME WARNER MERGER

To put this merger in context, it was at the very start of the Internet age, way back in 2003. AOL led the industry in developing an Internet presence with millions of subscribers expanding exponentially each month. It is a bit hard to understand in today's fully connected world, but establishing the ability to immediately reach millions of customers online in their own homes was unprecedented at the time. But even AOL was struggling with how to *monetize* the significant cost they had to invest in technology and marketing to build out this network. Having subscribers alone was of little value in a for-profit company like AOL if they could not figure out what goods and services to sell to this captive audience. Despite AOL's innovation and exponential subscriber growth, analysts were concerned about the revenue generation model that would allow AOL to become profitable in the long term.

While AOL was the definition of a new-age Internet company, Time Warner was a classic old-school organization. With a long history and conservative approach to business, Time Warner had developed a vast store of valuable hardcopy content in publishing, including film, TV, and magazines. But they lacked the online network that was forecast to replace the current distribution channels of this content by hardcopy magazines and newspapers. In January 2001, the companies completed a $350 billion merger that required $78 billion in acquisition debt. What better way to drive revenue synergies? Time Warner had the content, but no way to distribute it online. AOL had the online network, but lacked the content that people wanted to buy. This presented a classic opportunity for revenue synergies.

The deal sounded good in theory, but the results were a disaster. After the merger, AOL subscriber growth slowed. Time Warner's ad sales began to drop. The unprecedented revenue synergies suggested by the deal were very slow to materialize. The valuation bubble surrounding all Internet companies burst. In the end, two fundamentally good companies on a stand-alone basis had started to destroy value by merging. On January 13, 2003, AOL's CEO, Steven Case, the architect of the deal, was forced to resign due to "shareholder disappointment with the company and with me personally."

But even after Case resigned, the problems with the merged entity continued for over a decade. By January 2015, the fifteenth anniversary of the merger, the market value for AOL had fallen to $3.6 billion and Time Warner to $68.9 billion. (The companies had by that time separated again, realizing that it was simply too hard to work together.) This is compared to a $280 billion valuation for the combined AOL/Time Warner at the time of the acquisition, or a fall in value of over $200 billion over 15 years.[5] Time Warner had become the symbol of a failed acquisition.

What went wrong? Think about the type of culture of an old-economy company like Time Warner, based on the East Coast with a long legacy and conservative management team. Compare that to the culture of a West Coast start-up company with a younger workforce, casual dress code, and Ping Pong tables in the breakroom. As we mentioned earlier, driving revenue synergies can be very difficult unless buyer and seller are willing to collaborate to deliver them and customers are willing to respond positively. In the case of AOL Time Warner the company cultures never meshed, the customers did not embrace the concept, and two perfectly good companies on a stand-alone basis were ruined by combining.

This case highlights the importance of reviewing the culture of buyer and seller as part of the due diligence process. Revenue synergies are hard to quantify and deliver because they depend on qualitative factors such as customer preferences or employee culture and willingness to work together. Alternatively, cost synergies are easier to calculate and influence for things like the level of savings that would result from shrinking the workforce by 10 percent. But, because they are harder, deal teams often avoid looking objectively at the reasonableness of achieving the revenue synergies needed to make the deal successful. And by the time they realize they can't achieve these synergies, it is often too late.

An article in *Fortune* by Rita Gunther McGrath stated it perfectly:

> *Merging the cultures of the combined companies was problematic from the get go. Certainly the lawyers and professionals involved with the merger did the conventional due diligence on the numbers. What also needed to happen, and evidently didn't, was due diligence on the culture. The aggressive and, many said, arrogant AOL people "horrified" the more staid and corporate Time Warner side. Cooperation and promised synergies failed to materialize as mutual disrespect came to color their relationships.*[6]

WELLS FARGO BUYS WACHOVIA

Fast forward to October 2008, when Wells Fargo buys Wachovia, including the now-troubled consolidated operations of Golden West, for $15.1 billion. A key risk in Wachovia's original purchase of Golden West was "converting a thrift franchise like Golden West with only two products into a full-service bank like Wachovia with multiple product lines and a cross-selling of products among these lines." Clearly this was planned to be a major source of material revenue synergies to the deal.

And you can probably guess what happens next. These cross-selling practices, designed to create synergies between combining companies, ended up causing material problems for Wells Fargo and its CEO, John Stumpf. Here were the headlines at the time:

> "Wells Fargo Pulls Back on Cross Selling After Sales Scandal," *Fortune*, September 12, 2016

"What Created Wells Fargo Corrupt Cross-Selling Culture? Toxic Execs," *The Financial Brand*, April 2017

"Wells Fargo CEO to Face Senate Panel in Cross-Selling Scandal," Bloomberg, September 12, 2016

In 2016, it emerged that 5,300 Wells Fargo employees had created over two million fake deposit and credit card accounts for existing customers in order to achieve aggressive internal cross-selling targets. These targets were put in place to maximize the number of different Wells Fargo products each customer signed up for. As we explained earlier, adding product and distributing it to existing customers can be a primary driver of revenue synergies with very little incremental cost. In fact, it was mentioned as a key driver to the Golden West/Wachovia merger way back in 2008. But cross-selling revenue has to be done ethically and with the full consent of each and every customer impacted.

This final case highlights three of the lessons discussed in this chapter around due diligence, integration, and culture:

1. *The need to be especially careful of revenue synergies.* Synergies are often much harder to deliver than they may appear in the financial model. Wells Fargo is an unfortunate example of when pressure for results can result in unrealistic budgets that employees try to stretch too far to achieve.

2. *The importance of integration.* Golden West's practices may or may not have contributed to the cross-selling abuses ultimately uncovered after Wells Fargo bought Wachovia. However, introducing new procedures from a buyer to the target company is an area that needs to be carefully coordinated. Managed improperly, it can easily contribute to abuses. New employees of the target company are likely trying to make a good first impression, meet their financial targets, and, as a result, may be less likely to speak up when seeing questionable activities of the buyer, particularly if the bad practices have been in place for years with no consequences.

3. *The importance of culture.* One of the most damning criticisms of Wells Fargo was that with the magnitude of this problem, two million unauthorized accounts perpetrated by 5,300 separate employees, management either knew or should have known about the cross-selling problems. A 113-page postmortem report by Wells Fargo internal investigators concluded that Wells Fargo CEO John Stumpf "was by his nature an optimistic executive who refused to believe the sales model was seriously impaired."[7] A failure by senior management teams to root out and make an example of bad behavior can create a culture

where these things are allowed. The inference of this report was that senior management did know about the abusive cross-selling practices, but did little to correct them.

NOTES

1. Price was subsequently reduced to $21 billion based as it was on an all-stock deal.
2. *Frontline*, "Breaking the Bank," produced by Michael Kirk, Jim Gilmore, and Mike Wiser, June 16, 2009.
3. Ibid.
4. Punk Ziegel & Co., May 31, 2007.
5. *Bloomberg View*, "Lessons from the AOL Time Warner Disaster," by Katie Benner, January 14, 2015.
6. *Fortune*, "15 Years Later, Lessons from the Failed AOL-Time Warner Merger," by Rita Gunther McGrath, January 15, 2015.
7. *The Financial Brand*, "What Created Wells Fargo Corrupt Cross-Selling Culture? Toxic Execs," by Jeffery Pitcher, April 17, 2017.

CHAPTER 4

The Opportunities and Risks of Expanding Your Business Globally

What we know about the global financial crisis is that we don't know much.

—Paul Samuelson

As regional economies continue to globalize, expanding into foreign markets is a natural progression for companies that currently do business exclusively in their home markets. Access to new products and new customers allows firms to continue growing, particularly if they have already achieved a high share of their existing markets. There are many terrific examples of large firms that have successfully transitioned from purely domestic companies into global players. Companies such as General Electric, United Technologies, and Goldman Sachs have become truly international, not by vacating their domestic markets, but by taking their core competencies and expanding them overseas.

Firms often use an acquisition, partnership, or joint venture to expand globally. The idea is that by having a local partner it will be easier to understand each market and how they do business. What better way to understand the local customs and norms than by hiring people embedded in the country? An acquisition of a quality overseas company can be a quick way to gain scale in new markets in a prudent way. This is arguably a lot easier than trying to start an overseas business *de-novo* (i.e., from the ground up).

Think about what is required to start a business in a new country from the ground up. You first need to hire local employees. Many industries require a local license to do business that can take months to obtain. You would need to find office space and/or build new manufacturing facilities, develop a brand name, find customers, and so forth. And you need to do all of this in a foreign country, thousands of miles away, with a different culture, customs, and language. While it can be done, it is a detailed and time-consuming process that can take months or even years to fully assimilate and build a profitable business.

Alternatively, a merger or acquisition can be very tempting. It can provide an immediate presence with scale in new foreign markets. You don't have to take the time to hire a sales force or management team. You don't have to go through the lengthy approval process for local licenses that could be particularly hard to obtain for a foreign investor. You don't have to spend the time and cost associated with building out a brand name. This can make it look especially appealing to buy into the new country immediately versus building a presence over time.

However, the risks of expanding overseas via M&A are frequently discounted. As hard as purely domestic business combinations are, mergers and acquisitions in a global context are significantly more complicated. Differences in cultures and norms can make it very hard for the two parties to communicate. Local regulations and political structures add even more complexity. Although M&A provides a faster entry point to a new country, it is normally much more expensive to buy a company than to build one from the bottom up. Most sellers will demand a significant premium to today's true market value for a profitable, well-run company. They will, understandably, expect a premium to compensate them for all of the time and effort they put in to build the organization from the ground up. So, while an immediate acquisition may seem very appealing and oftentimes work out well, international M&A can have horrible consequences to both firms if not managed properly.

In this chapter, we will use the example of a large Norwegian telecommunications company, Telenor, merging with a much smaller Indian company, Unitech, to show some of the critical mistakes to avoid when expanding into foreign countries. We present a detailed analysis of the events leading up to, during, and following the Telenor merger from several years ago for two reasons. First is to show the at times mundane, at other times significant, distractions to a management team that can be caused by trying to build an overseas presence. Cross-border investments are not necessarily bad. In fact, many work out extraordinarily well. But management teams frequently underestimate the distraction and risk that such expansive strategies can have for their core business.

Second is to illustrate the fact that many if not all of the issues facing cross-border deals from 15 years ago are the same issues businesses face today in international expansion. It is amazing how management teams fail to learn from the past. The tendency is always to think that my deal is "different from those other deals" that did not work. Inexperienced buyers will oftentimes go into deals a bit too self-confident, only to fall into traps experienced by other teams time and time again over decades of M&A activity—in this case close to 20 years ago! We will use the Telenor JV to illustrate the commonsense problems that, if they can be avoided, will dramatically improve the chances of a successful cross-border deal. We end the chapter with a summary of the lessons learned from the Telenor case and a discussion of future trends expected in cross-border M&A.

TELENOR INDIA JOINT VENTURE

The joint venture between Norwegian telecommunication company Telenor and Indian real estate group Unitech is a good example of the difficulties that can be posed when trying to expand too quickly into new geographies.

Following is a relatively detailed outline of the events leading up to and subsequent to this joint venture. The detail is included to show how complicated these transactions can be and the distraction that they can cause to the core markets of both parties if not managed properly. In any complicated cross-border transaction such as this, it is critical for management to remain focused on their domestic markets that have driven their success to date. Being too concerned with expansion into new, unfamiliar territories, at the risk of protecting the existing strengths of the company, can end up destroying material company value.

At the time of the joint venture, Telenor was the seventh largest global telecommunications operator in the world with over 190 million subscribers in its consolidated subsidiaries. The company started in Norway in 1855 as a state monopoly and developed into a multinational corporation that became a public company in 1994. Its main operations were focused on three geographies:

1. *Nordic countries.* Telenor was the incumbent and leading provider of mobile communications in Norway, with a history of more than 150 years. In Denmark the company was the largest mobile operator, and it was the third largest in Sweden. In 2010, these three countries accounted for 53 percent of revenues and 64 percent of operating cash flows, which clearly established Telenor's Nordic operations as its most important, but also the most mature business segment. While company management felt it was critical to protect their core Nordic markets, they had an overarching goal of being a truly global company.

2. *Central and Eastern Europe.* Telenor was the second largest of three mobile operators in Hungary, number two in Serbia, and the largest of three players in Montenegro. Telenor also held a minority stake in VimpelCom, the second largest mobile operator in Russia in terms of subscriptions.

3. *Asia.* In Asia, Telenor was the second largest telecommunications player in Thailand and Pakistan and a leading player in Malaysia and Bangladesh. Telenor's obvious gap in its Asia coverage was in addressing the billion-plus population of India. To be truly global, this was a gap that management believed they absolutely had to fill. But the company now had a decision to make: How to get into India in the most effective way without distracting management from the successful parts of their business.

Telenor had a long history of expanding geographically via partnerships and acquisitions. Rather than trying to go into India on their own, management decided that a joint venture with an existing in-country provider would be faster and provide immediate scale in this critical market for the company. A domestic Indian company called Unitech seemed like the perfect partner in the wireless space. Unitech had previously been awarded wireless telephone licenses for most of India, and they knew the industry and the country well. For Telenor, a relationship with Unitech provided an opportunity for a new nationwide mobile network in a country they had wanted to enter for years.

Unitech Wireless was a much smaller company than Telenor. It was founded in 2007 as a start-up mobile operator by Unitech Group, the second largest real estate group in India. Earlier in 2008 it had been one of the few local players to win an Indian license and spectrum for 13 regions. In its 2008 annual report the management stated, "While there are some synergies with real estate, the telecom business is new to Unitech. Your Company, therefore, intends to get a partner who primarily brings in cutting-edge technology and industry expertise, and jointly develop the project."[1] While a much younger company than Telenor, Unitech had established a material presence in India with valuable assets. A joint venture providing capital, industry expertise, and the extensive global network of Telenor might have seemed very attractive to the smaller and less mature management team of Unitech at this time.

TELENOR'S GLOBAL STRATEGY OVER TIME

In the 1990s, Telenor was in a strong position to expand its communication services internationally, and expansion had become a core strategy of the company. The company claimed to have a material head start on technology and therefore felt an obligation to transfer knowledge to new partners and markets abroad. Many of the telecommunication solutions they provided were flexible enough to be implemented across national borders and in diverse countries. Management viewed this as a unique competitive advantage.

Telenor's geographical mix of revenues became increasingly diversified across Europe and Asia, notably in Greece, Ireland, Germany, Austria (1997), Ukraine (1998), Denmark (2000), and Hungary (2002). As such, revenue and subscriber growth in Telenor's operations was mainly driven by customer growth and increased use of mobile services in emerging markets. In 2005, Telenor had already become the world's twelfth largest mobile company, and a short three years later it climbed to seventh largest.

Telenor had historically focused on start-up of greenfield mobile operations (i.e., de novo) to expand internationally. In the 1990s, the company had established a track record of building new businesses with a long-term approach to investment. Telenor would also consider minority positions in an M&A process, as long they saw a clear route to building control, in other words, owning a majority of the company over time. Telenor had demonstrated a steady, yet cautious, approach to M&A in most of its markets, with the one exception being Eastern Europe where they had encountered significant problems.

TELENOR EXPANDS INTO EASTERN EUROPE

In 1993, Telenor expanded into Central and Eastern Europe, first by taking over a company called Pannon in Hungary. The company made further steps in Central and Eastern Europe and signed a contract for the development of satellite networks in the Czech Republic. During the following years, Telenor invested in joint ventures in Lithuania, Montenegro, and Austria.

Telenor entered the Russian market in early 1993 by acquiring wireless cell phone licenses for the city of St. Petersburg. It was an entry point to a market that afforded incredible potential. But it was not until 1998 that Telenor finalized two acquisition moves that would become the basis for its development in both the Russian and Ukrainian market. Telenor signed a contract to acquire a 35 percent ownership stake in Kyivstar Wireless in Ukraine for $40 million. In December of that year, Telenor signed an agreement to acquire a 25 percent stake in VimpelCom, which at the time was nearly bankrupt with only 130,000 customers.

In October 2004, a significant conflict erupted between the two partners. VimpelCom's management proposed to acquire URS WellCom, a small and loss-making Ukrainian mobile operator. After analyzing the company, Telenor concluded that the price asked for the company, $231 million, was too high, especially given that the company would require large subsequent investments. Telenor requested the identity of the sellers, but they were denied. This was a red flag as VimpelCom was unwilling to disclose the identity of the seller, but there was no logical reason not to. As 90 percent or more of the shareholders had to vote in favor of the motion, Telenor's refusal stopped the acquisition of URS WellCom.

But Telenor's refusal to move forward, although allowed under the board resolutions, was not well received by VimpelCom. Victor Makarenko, a shareholder understood to hold only two shares in VimpelCom, launched three lawsuits against Telenor, aiming to annul the shareholders' agreement of VimpelCom and to implore VimpelCom to acquire URS WellCom. In the Ukraine, another major shareholder called Alfa Group started a four-year-long boycott of the board of directors, and refused to appear at shareholders' meetings. This meant that no shareholders' meetings could be held as Ukrainian law requires attendance from at least 60 percent in order to achieve quorum.

In 2006, Telenor initiated three different lawsuits in Moscow in an effort to overturn the URS acquisition. *Telenor v. Kyivstar* (2006) resulted in a ruling by the Ukrainian court that declared "the shareholders' agreement null and void in its entirety under Ukrainian law."[2] Ukrainian lawsuits involving Telenor continued; further rulings prevented Ernst & Young from performing audits, eventually forcing Telenor to remove Kyivstar from its financial accounts. In August 2007, Telenor finally won a total victory in the arbitration proceeding in New York against its Alfa Group subsidiary, in connection with the violations of the shareholders' agreement in Kyivstar, ordering Alfa to return to all shareholders and board meetings.

Although Telenor ultimately won the lawsuit, this is a perfect example of the potential unintended consequences of a failed acquisition. Pursuing a "small loss-making Ukrainian mobile operator" that would have little material impact on the overall results of the company, even if it had closed, caused a four-year-long distraction to the board of directors. It may have been very tempting to expand further into the Ukraine with a company like URS WellCom at the time. But in hindsight, the potential rewards of pursuing this relatively small acquisition were clearly not worth the associated risks and management distraction from pursuing it.

And the conflict related to this small distracting acquisition was still not over. In the spring of 2008, Telenor was informed of yet another lawsuit launched by the small VimpelCom shareholder Farimex based in the British Virgin Isles, claiming $2.8 billion for the same reason related to the acquisition. The claim was later raised to $5.7 billion. The Siberian court sided with Farimex, and ruled that Telenor would have to pay $2.8 billion in compensation, not to Farimex, but to VimpelCom! Telenor appealed the decision, but the Court of Appeals responded only by lowering the compensation that Telenor would have to pay to $1.7 billion.

Moreover, a Russian bailiff acting on behalf of Farimex seized all of Telenor's shares in VimpelCom and put a freeze on its assets, even though Telenor had not been officially served with any claim. It was only in late 2009 that Telenor and Altimo announced their agreement to combine their assets in Kyivstar and VimpelCom into a new Bermuda-registered company, VimpelCom Ltd, with its headquarters in the Netherlands. This finally ended the continued conflict around this company.

Despite all of the unfortunate M&A activity and subsequent distractions in Eastern Europe, Telenor management continued to emphasize a shift in its global corporate strategy toward even more growth through profitable acquisitions. Their stated reasons for pursuing more M&A activity were a superior governance structure and highly experienced management team, expected global procurement synergies, expected contribution to the consolidated value of the company, and an increase in the importance of being in different geographies.[3] This was a risky move for any company, particularly one with a successful track record of building companies relative to a rather mixed history of trying to purchase them in Eastern Europe.

TELENOR PUSHES INTO ASIA

Nevertheless, Telenor was determined to continue pushing its international strategy, and its next target was Asia. The company argued that it had learned from these mistakes and as a result would be more effective buying or joint venturing with another party going forward. This raises some interesting questions. Should Telenor have pressed on with their global ambitions after their problems in Eastern Europe? Had they really learned their lesson? Could they apply what they learned in Eastern Europe to a very different M&A environment in Asia?

Although it has improved in recent years, at the time, India was a notoriously difficult country to do business in as a foreign corporation. The government was at times reluctant to let foreign companies into critical infrastructure areas such as media and telecom. There had been instances of new, punitive laws and taxes being implemented against foreign investors and then applied retroactively to the time they entered the country with little or no explanation of the rationale. Why was Telenor so anxious to get into India so shortly after the issues they faced in Russia under very similar arrangements?

But Telenor had confidence in Asia and had built a position as a leading mobile operator in the region. In fact, Telenor Group added more than 23 million subscribers to Asia in 2010, making Asia the highest growth region of the entire group. At the end of 2010, Telenor Group's five Asian operations generated 39 percent of the group's total revenues. It was also in a strong position in terms of its share in all of its markets, in line with its stated objective to be a market leader in all countries where it chose to do business.

Telenor also saw great potential in the growing economy of Pakistan, home to the sixth largest population of the world. It acquired a license in 2004 for NOK 1.8 billion ($210 million) and was able to roll out its service in just 11 months. Though it entered the Pakistani market as it was suffering from general revenue declines, the overall results of the global strategy allowed Telenor to enjoy its first year of positive cash flow in 2007 while achieving 20 percent market share in 2008.

Telenor believed that a difficult regulatory environment could actually provide opportunities given the growing size and scale of their operations relative to smaller, local competitors in Pakistan. In their presentation to the analysts in 2005, management outlined the regulatory environment and the highly competitive landscape that would present medium-term challenges, but also opportunities to growing a profitable business in Pakistan. Average revenue per minute had decreased over 200 percent in the previous seven years and, while that rate of decline was not unheard of within a developing market, stabilizing this decline would be essential to offset the reductions in revenue. Telenor was able to achieve remarkable increases in the number of subscribers, doubling its customer base in 2006 and again in 2007 and achieving a 33 percent growth rate in 2008. This gave company management a lot of comfort that they could have great success in India.

Telenor viewed a joint venture with Unitech in India as a unique opportunity to enter one of the world's largest and fastest growing mobile markets. India had the world's second largest population of 1.2 billion people, and was also the world's largest untapped market at the time, with a mobile penetration materially lower than China's. In India, only 30 percent of the population was urbanized with almost 800 million people who were not connected. Telenor believed that their investment would be supported by growth in the Indian market, irrespective of any market share gains they would be able to achieve, and that increasing demand from Indian start-up businesses would offset cyclical slowdowns for more established operations.

Telenor planned for a low-cost operational model, light in assets and based on the outsourcing of key services such as IT. With the general goal of quickly rolling out its mobile network, Telenor's initial business plan included a launch of mobile service in the middle of 2009 through instant access to 50,000 existing sites via tower sharing agreements. The signing of tower sharing agreements would simultaneously lower Telenor's barriers to entry and reduce capital expenditure through access to an existing, well-established infrastructure. Through these agreements, Telenor estimated it could expand its network in half the time it took to accomplish in Pakistan. Management believed that any negative up-front impact to costs from this approach would be more than offset by the long-term revenue benefits.

The attractiveness of India's population was complemented by the positive macroeconomic features of the country. India was a rapidly developing economy, with GDP per capita expected to double over the subsequent decade, thereby contributing to an absolute increase in mobile spending and the number of people who would become mobile users and subscribers. For example, Telenor represented that net additions for the 12 months ended December 31, 2008, had been over 10 million users monthly.

Management believed that they could effectively roll out their existing Asian business model in India with a focus on an attractive brand, a quality product, and a strong local presence while leveraging their extensive experience in greenfield projects and controlling positions in key joint ventures or alliances elsewhere in the world. The Indian market was underpenetrated, growing, and, given its high churn rates, open to new entrants in search of market share gains. Telenor's intentions as presented to the investors in February 2009 were to put to use "proven concepts from other Asian markets including excellence in distribution, target offerings to over one million pan-Indian customers, subscriber lifecycle management, and building a strong organization and brand."[4]

This is a classic mistake made by many companies looking to expand internationally. Assuming the management methods and marketing techniques that were successful in one Asian country will simply transfer seamlessly to another Asian country is often a recipe for disaster. In this case, the difference in local licensing requirements, user behavior, and in-country pricing anomalies made investing in India unique to anywhere else in the world Telenor had previously tried to penetrate. By assuming all of Asia was the same, management underestimated the integration issues they would face with this joint venture. Doing business in India clearly presented the company with a host of new challenges that it had not encountered in Pakistan.

As we now know, the Asian region includes vastly differing cultures, markets, and norms of behavior. Doing business in China could not be more different than doing business in India or doing business in Thailand. Telenor made a critical mistake in assuming that a wireless business model rolled out in Russia or Pakistan would fit perfectly into the unique cultural and business environment posed by India. This is a common pitfall to many global M&A strategies. While it sounds like common sense, many fail to fully appreciate the subtle differences among countries in the same region. This can become particularly acute when trying to execute on a complicated, cross-border agreement between two companies that have never known each other.

THE TELENOR UNITECH JOINT VENTURE

The deal was announced on October 28, 2008, with an expected closing by year end. The deal was contingent on the signing of cell phone tower sharing agreements and local regulatory approval. Telenor was to take a 60 percent stake in Unitech for an equity contribution of $1.1 billion. The proposed operating agreement was that Telenor would assume financial and operating control in the business. Telenor offered to fund the transaction with a NOK 12 billion ($1.1 billion) issue of new shares in the first quarter of 2009 while keeping the dividend policy unchanged. Both companies believed that the tower sharing agreements provided an important strategic and operational advantage by reducing the barriers to entry and helping lower capital expenditures. However, the competition was intense with three other new licensees and a large number of more established regional and national operators.

The public markets did not like the deal. The announcement led to a one-day decline of 26 percent in Telenor's share price, or an approximate loss of $2.7 billion in equity value. The average broker target price was reduced by over 30 percent, and S&P and Moody's both issued a negative watch on Telenor's credit rating. Several brokerage research houses commented that not only would India's market be unhelpful to Telenor, but an expansion into India would actually destroy value in the company. Morgan Stanley, in a report published in January 2009, stated that it remained cautious on management's projections for this acquisition.[5]

Clearly, the market as a whole did not agree with what management believed it could do with an Indian operation, despite Telenor's success in other areas throughout Asia. Did the press and analysts know more about the dangers of international expansion than Telenor management? Despite considerable pressure from shareholders and a falling stock price, Telenor was convinced that it should move forward on the deal and get into the Indian market. In its 2008 annual report, Telenor's CEO once again acknowledged the shareholders' concerns about the deal, but restated the plan as follows:

> *Telenor's decision to enter India has received reactions from its shareholders. While understanding the different opinions around this, given the current global financial crisis, I want to underline Telenor's long term industrial history and focus. Entering the Indian mobile market represents a unique opportunity to take part in one of the fastest growing telecom markets in the world and leverage on Telenor's proven green field expertise and experience. The entry into India fits strongly with our industrial strategy, and I firmly believe that it will create long-term shareholder value.[6]*

Despite continued negative reactions from stakeholders and analysts, management was firm in their conviction. The deal eventually went ahead with a revised funding structure, helped by an endorsement by the Norwegian government, which held a 54 percent stake in the company at the time. In March 2009, Telenor and Unitech formally agreed to proceed with the joint venture. In September of that year, Unitech was rebranded as Unicor. Unicor launched its initial services in eight regions of India in December 2009. Another five regions were introduced in June 2010, expanding Unicor's coverage to 40 percent of India's population. However, Telenor faced two main challenges in India from the very beginning of this venture: An extremely competitive landscape and regulatory uncertainty that affected operational capabilities.

At the time they entered the market, there were already four players with nationwide networks and several other regional players who were expanding aggressively. Unicor's India managing director stated, "The competitive levels in India are very high, and we want to show we are capable of surviving in this market. So it is more or less on Telenor's pride. Despite the skepticism of many people, we are determined to make it work here." This was the first sign of weakness around the prospects for this newly established joint venture. Such comments stating that all we are doing is trying to survive are never a good sign, particularly when they are made right after an acquisition is agreed to.

On the regulatory side, Telenor was surprised by how difficult it became to acquire wireless spectrum. By 2010, Telenor had still not received new spectrum from the government institutions in key cities. This caused the company to delay spending capital in these areas and to focus instead on areas where the spectrum was available. Again, a common issue with cross-border deals, given increasing levels of nationalism around the globe, gaining access to key assets like wireless spectrum, marine ports, real estate, key technology, and so on is increasingly being resisted by the home countries. Governments are becoming more and more reluctant to let the "crown jewels" of their countries fall into the hands of foreign businesses.

To make matters worse, Telenor became involved in a highly visible scandal around misappropriation of wireless spectrum by senior government officials. Although these allegations were made about events preceding the joint venture, Telenor was included in the litigation. In April 2010, India's Central Bureau of Investigation filed charges against local parties for corruption, including Unicor. Telenor became one of only two foreign firms brought into this litigation, which ultimately could have resulted in a suspension of their license to do business in the entire country.

The head of Telenor's India operations rationalized, "When Telenor Group entered into India, the country had a well-defined regulatory and political framework for the development of the Indian telecom sector. We predicted that India would be a very competitive market, but we could not foresee the regulatory and political turmoil the telecom industry is facing today." However, this explanation did little to mitigate the damage caused to Telenor's financial position and its shareholders from this ill-advised joint venture.

POSTMORTEM ON THE TELENOR UNITECH JOINT VENTURE

What has happened to Telenor in India since starting out with such strong projections for success? The head of Telenor's operations in Asia, Sigve Brekke, had predicted that Unitech Wireless would cover half of India by the end of 2010. The deal was supposed to be the breakthrough the company needed to penetrate the massive Indian market. But management ultimately faced serious challenges in assimilating Unitech into Telenor while trying to compete with long-established Indian mobile carriers such as Airtel, Vodafone, and Idea.

Fast forward to 2016, and Telenor announced that not only would they stop participating in spectrum auctions for new regions in India, but that they might withdraw from the country altogether as they were struggling to secure additional network capacity for affordable prices.[7] The competition continued to increase, driving up the price of spectrum auctions and compressing margins. As of this writing, a main competitor, Bharti Airtel, has been negotiating with Telenor Unitech about buying half of Telenor India for a depressed price $350 million. The comments from management and change in sentiment around this deal from a very optimistic start to the current discussions around a "depressed" sale price are remarkable. Clearly, the problems of technology, business operations, and cultural assimilation have proved not wholly surmountable for Telenor.

This case is a great example of the risks posed by entering new markets, even with a local partner to help with the transition. It is one thing to talk about an M&A strategy as being "complex" and another to go through the detailed work of integration, regulation, and license approval, all while dealing with material changes in market dynamics over the years. For example, as we see in this case, simple things like a favorable court ruling in New York do not necessarily mean a favorable ruling on the exact same facts in a court in Siberia. Local rules and customs can dramatically influence outcomes that at times defy common sense.

Although the rewards of going global can be significant and many firms have succeeded, the downside can be considerable. Becoming a global company sounds appealing and often seems like the right course of action as "everyone" is doing it. But a deal that goes bad can be a massive distraction to one's core business and result in a distraction for years to come.

LESSONS LEARNED

Despite a poor record of international expansion via M&A, Telenor insisted on pushing forward into India. It seems that management lost perspective and became overly enamored with being a global company without fully considering the impact it could have on its core operations. This case illustrates several lessons to keep in mind when attempting to expand into foreign countries:

■ *Don't underestimate the risks.* Foreign acquisitions and joint ventures can be extremely risky. When entering new regions with different business cultures and norms—even with a good partner—the risk of executing your agenda according to plan is very difficult.

■ *Beware of regulatory changes.* As we saw with Telenor, it is extremely hard to anticipate changes to regulations in all of the regions where you do business. Regulations can change quickly, without rationale, and have an immediate, significant impact on in-country operations.

■ *New ventures are difficult.* In Chapter 2, we examined several benefits of building a business from the bottom up versus buying a mature property. But you should not underestimate the challenges of a build strategy in a foreign market. Cash flows in a start-up are normally negative in the early years until you can build scale. Patience and commitment to long-term viability is critical to the venture's success.

■ *Pay attention to your shareholders and analysts.* Telenor resisted the strong criticism from shareholders and the analyst community when this Indian joint venture was announced. Any CEO has a variety of stakeholders whose views should be taken into consideration as these constituencies have a vested interest in a positive outcome to any business combination.

■ *Learn from your mistakes.* Telenor clearly had a tough time in the Eastern European expansion it pursued via M&A. The firm was a bit overconfident about its ability to expand essentially the same business plan into a competitive Indian market. But problems with M&A in one country can easily expand into others. This needs to be considered.

■ *Don't underestimate your competition.* As an outsider looking into a new market it may seem easy to compete. However, you must consider that many of the existing players have decades of experience in these markets. Competitive advantages can be created by new entrants over time. But simply assuming that all current market participants are ineffective and can be beaten is a very dangerous strategy indeed. Management must closely evaluate what they can bring to the market and how difficult it will be to differentiate their company from longstanding, local competition.

■ *Reputational risk.* Truly global companies will be judged not just by how they act in their home countries, but by how they behave in every region where they operate. A parent company can be impacted by the actions of any subsidiary, no matter how remote or in what jurisdiction. For example, being one of only two foreign firms implicated in the Indian wireless spectrum corruption charges put Telenor in a very difficult position. In these cases, it is not always the scale of the business or the size of the issue that matters. It is the potential reputational risk from such events to the global franchise. A formal charge of corruption, no matter how limited, can have a material effect on your firm's reputation and ability to do business going forward.

- *Differences in standards of care.* Imagine that you are a U.S.-headquartered corporation doing business in Vietnam. Should you be held to the level of care of the parent company or the local customs in Vietnam, which may be very different from those of the parent's home base? For example, in some countries "facilitation payments" are common to local officials or business partners to accelerate obtaining licenses or closing transactions. But under U.S. law, corporations are held to regulations such as the Foreign Corrupt Practices Act, which specifically forbid such payments. And there are criminal penalties to management for violating them. Therefore, you need to ensure that your partner will uphold this more stringent standard of care even though your competition may not. This could make it hard for your subsidiary to remain competitive by being forced to obey restrictions not imposed by other local firms in the industry.
- *Spend adequate time due-diligencing your partner.* You can simply never do enough due diligence when deciding whom to partner with in a foreign country. You need to spend time with the counterparty, do adequate referencing, and get comfortable that your partner will work with the same level of corporate social responsibility as you require. The culture, integrity, and way of doing business of your partner can make all the difference as you decide to expand globally.
- *Don't let foreign activities distract you from your core business.* As we saw in the Telenor case, foreign acquisitions can be complex and time consuming. People tend to migrate to exciting new deals, but often at the expense of doing their day jobs. Some companies will create temporary deal teams to focus on an acquisition while a second team remains centered on maintaining and growing the core business. Balancing between a stable core business and taking calculated risks to expand globally are absolutely critical to the success of any venture.

The ultimate outcome of Telenor's expansion into India has yet to be determined. However, the significant issues to date highlight the risks of international expansion. Senior management must weigh the rewards of global expansion with the risks of doing so. But regardless of the industry or the country, keeping certain fundamental principles in mind can vastly improve your company's chances for success.

TRENDS FOR THE FUTURE

Larger Asian-headquartered companies, particularly those from China and India, continue to aggressively enter the European and U.S. markets via acquisition. These firms are looking to gain exposure to new markets, as well as diversify and acquire brands that can be marketed back home. Additionally, they want access to the natural resources needed to meet domestic demand, as well as to accumulate intellectual, technical, and marketing knowledge. It is anticipated that China will become the largest cross-border investor by the end of this decade. Chinese global offshore assets are expected to increase from $6.4 trillion today to over $20 trillion by 2020. Many Chinese companies are looking to North America and Europe when considering M&A, as the slowdown in their home markets continues.

The $1.8 billion purchase of Ford's Volvo automakers by Chinese company Geely is a good example of this trend. Through this purchase, Geely gained access to new technology, entry into the U.S. automobile market, and the Volvo brand name, which could be marketed in China. Global acquisitions such as these are not done simply on the basis of achieving a desired return. Rather, they include strategic considerations that outweigh the pure economics and provide longer-term value to firms like Geely and to the overall Chinese economy.

Chinese firms have also started to broaden their attention beyond raw materials and heavy industrial sectors. Food is a key industry that Chinese firms are becoming more interested in, specifically sugar, protein, and dairy. For example, Brightgoods, a Chinese firm, is expected to take some of Australian Manassen's brands and launch them in China as a premium brand name. Premium brands are becoming more popular in China among an increasingly affluent middle class living in the central cities. Buying established names from other countries provides an immediate and well-known premium brand immediately, and saves the firm the time and cost associated with trying to develop a brand over time.

While China seems to be driving a lot of the growth in cross-border deals today, other Eastern firms started their global ties with the West long ago. For example, the large Indian conglomerate Tata established a presence in London way back in 1907 to buy raw materials for its Indian operations. In 1975, Tata formed an outsourcing business, Tata Consultancy Services, that pioneered the outsourcing of computer processing to India.

But Tata's big jump from India to the United States was through its purchase of Tetley Tea in 2000. Global expansion was only part of the reason for the Tetley deal. Tata also wanted to learn about brands and how to develop them. Tetley had started as a black tea, then went to more up-market green teas, and finally, to premium, luxury brand teas. This was the perfect platform for Tata not only to expand the awareness of their company overseas quickly, but also to learn about brand management.

The company later took over Corus Steel and Jaguar Land Rover. In each case Tata was buying a bigger, more established firm. These acquisitions provided a means for Tata to continue to grow internationally on an increasingly large scale. They also provided immediate name recognition for Tata in the Western world to match their quality, well-known name in India. Developing the Tata brand name outside of India without the acquisition of already established firms would have taken years to accomplish. Tata's purchase of Land Rover provided immediate access to an established brand name and Land Rover's valuable, off-road technology, which Tata could also leverage in its home market. The company's purchase of Corus allowed Tata to keep up with other large firms going global via acquisitions like Mittal Steel and gave it immediate access to an internationally renowned steel business.

If the past few years are any indication, Eastern companies will have an increasing influence in global M&A markets. In 2016 alone, cross-border deals into and out of India reached a six-year high of $56.2 billion, an 87 percent increase over the prior year. We will continue to see cross-border deals going both into and out of Asia. Western firms will want access to the growing, middle-class population of the East. Eastern firms will continue to expand west for access to brands, raw materials, and the technologies that can be brought back to their domestic markets. Mergers, acquisitions, and joint ventures can all be very effective means of expansion, but only if handled properly.

NOTES

1. 2008 Telenor Annual Report.
2. Storm Mem. in Opposition to the Telenor Mot. for Prelim. Injunc. Relief at 27.
3. 2007 Telenor Annual Report.
4. Telenor Investor Report, Feb. 2009.
5. 2009 Morgan Stanley Analyst Report.
6. 2008 Telenor Annual Report.
7. ET Bureau, *Economic Times/India Times*, "Telenor to Not Participate in Upcoming Spectrum Auctions," July 20, 2010, http://economictimes.indiatimes.com/news/company/corporate-trends/telenor-to-not-participate-in-upcoming-spectrum-auction/articleshow/53292820.cms.

CHAPTER 5

Culture Is Critical

Bankers cannot afford to be concerned with only the economic aspects of projects. There may be serious implications on the natural environment, the urban environment, on human culture.
—Arthur Erickson, Canadian architect

A CASE STUDY FROM CHINA

I remember it like it was yesterday. We had worked for many months to establish a renminbi (RMB)–denominated private equity fund with a major Chinese municipality. As a European investor, buying companies in China was becoming difficult without a local fund. Most of the Chinese entrepreneurs wanted local currency in exchange for investment into their companies. Due to local restrictions, it was hard if not impossible to convert the U.S. dollar, pound, or euro currencies into the RMB that sellers could use locally. Although we had been quite successful historically, this was starting to impede our ability to make quality investments in China.

Many of the second-tier cities in China were attempting to attract foreign capital to help grow their infrastructure and economies. From our side, even those provinces that were considered second tier by Chinese standards had the sheer population size and explosive economic growth to make them some of the most attractive places to invest in the world. From the Chinese side, access to large, sophisticated international investors from the West was viewed as a good way to help fund this growth. Connecting the available capital with the need for it on the ground via this local fund seemed like a natural progression.

Our team on the ground in China, based in Beijing, had worked for months with this province on the overall concept and the specific terms and conditions. The joint venture was critical to us, not just for currency reasons but for the opportunity it created. It gave us instant credibility in-country, and the provincial government could facilitate access to the hundreds of small-to-midsize companies that needed capital. By co-branding our product we were not viewed suspiciously as just another foreign investor but one who had come to agreeable terms with a local government.

Our progress thus far on the deal was a direct result of having people in-country who spoke the language and understood local laws and customs. We could have never accomplished this much from Europe alone. While it took longer than I had ideally wanted, we had taken the proper amount of time to cultivate the relationships in-country to get us to the brink of closing it.

The final meeting in the province was set for a Thursday in September with my local team scheduled to attend. On Tuesday, I received a call in our

London headquarters from our managing director on the ground in Beijing that I "had" to be at this meeting. My immediate reaction was to do whatever I could to help, but my daughter Rachel's birthday was that Thursday. I really didn't see the criticality for me to personally attend. I hated having to miss one of my daughter's birthdays, especially when I had a perfectly sound team on the ground in China. But the MD insisted that I personally attend, and this was a critical deal for us, so I agreed to go.

After calling my wife and daughter to sincerely apologize, I boarded a plane from Heathrow Airport to Beijing with a connection from Beijing to our partner's province. After a ten-hour flight to Beijing and another three-hour connection, I arrived just in time for the meeting. I was introduced to the provincial governor, who did not speak English, and I did not speak Mandarin. We said hello through an interpreter and entered the meeting.

The PowerPoint presentation and entire meeting was conducted in Mandarin. I sat there for an hour and tried to look attentive and not fall asleep after a long plane ride and time change. After the one-hour meeting ended, I packed up my briefcase, gave my regards to the leaders, exchanged business cards, boarded a plane back home, and waited for word on the final outcome. On Saturday morning our managing director in China called, thanking me profusely and relaying the good news that our deal was agreed to.

So what happened? I flew over 24 hours in a two-day period to be at a meeting where I clearly added no value. Did I miss my daughter's birthday for nothing? The true answer lies in the differences between American and Chinese cultures. As an American, I did not see the value in my trip. I assumed the Chinese already knew we were serious and the deal had the support of the executive team in London. I had reviewed the transaction with our corporate investment committee and had approval to move forward. The local team in China was clearly empowered to close the deal. But to our Chinese partner, my making the effort to be at this meeting was a sign of respect. I had the important "Chairman" business card, and I was based at the home office. My physical presence sent the message that:

- I, and my company, cared about the deal.
- This was an important meeting and the "decision maker" was in attendance to formally close the transaction after months of negotiations.
- I respected our counterparty enough to make the effort to be there.
- Our local people in China had the visibility and support from the senior management from the home office.

Another way to look at this was the type of message it would have sent if I did not bother to attend. Regardless of the cultural implications, what message would this imply to our counterparty? It may have signaled that:

- We did not care that much about the deal.
- I thought I was too important relative to our counterparty to make such a trip worthwhile.
- I was too busy with other pressing matters that I viewed as more important than our RMB fund.

In essence, it would have shown a lack of respect that could have derailed the months of work invested to get to this point in the process.

Leaders often have to make tough choices between professional demands and balancing their family life. Some of the decisions are easy— mandatory board meetings, time-pressured deals, regulatory deadlines, and so on. But some are more a matter of judgment. In this case it would have been very easy to rationalize why the work demand was not pressing. Culture has no hard-and-fast rules like other obligations. But the purpose of this chapter is to impress upon the reader that, despite being fluid and hard to define, attention to culture is as important as any other element of a successful deal integration. As an aside, I am proud to say that this is the *only* birthday of any of my three daughters that I have ever missed. But Rachel still does remember that I was not there for her on that special day.

This is just one example of many I could draw on to show the importance of understanding the culture of your counterparty in any M&A transaction. Even deals done in the same country can have massive cultural implications. Take the case of AOL/Time Warner we discussed in Chapter 3. It was the clash between the staid bricks-and-mortar culture of Time Warner and the entrepreneurial, young, Internet culture of AOL that ultimately caused the demise of this deal. In most deals, the buyer will engage a host of lawyers, accountants, consultants, and investment bankers to evaluate the target company. More time is probably spent on the financial model than any other element of the transaction. But it is often having the common sense around culture that can have the biggest impact.

This case in China also highlights the importance of having people on the ground in the countries you plan to invest in. For example, can you imagine me, as a six-foot-four American, getting off a plane in Beijing and trying to set up an RMB-denominated fund with a Chinese municipality? I did not know the local language or culture. I had no previous contact with municipalities or sense of how to structure this type of transaction. Fortunately, we had hired a solid team on the ground with that invaluable perspective. By having both local expertise along with access to Western capital we were able to build an effective partnership.

Many of the investments we did internationally were minority investments with local partners for just that reason. We would not take over the entire company. Rather, we would invest in a minority of the company for cash. This provided the seller with liquidity and access to our financial expertise, and it provided us with the local content and connections that were critical in-country. Our interests were aligned to do everything possible to grow the company we now jointly owned while using local expertise to make sure we stayed in full compliance with local laws and regulations.

There is an increasing trend today for the flow of capital cross-border, with a particularly increasing investment from Eastern countries into the West. Key strategic assets from ports and railways to trophy residential assets like the Plaza Hotel in New York City are increasingly being bought by Eastern investors. While there has been a recent backlash due to more sensitivity around protecting national assets, I do not see this trend slowing down. It will heighten the importance of sensitivity, on both sides, to the culture of your counterparty and how to drive the best outcome possible by understanding its significant potential impact.

A CASE STUDY FROM JAPAN

The impact of culture is at least as important after the deal closes as before. At one of my companies we completed the cross-border purchase of a large Japanese financial institution. We were concerned with an acquisition so far away from our headquarters in New York and how we would influence the management team to deliver the synergies and growth we had assumed in the acquisition projections. But we also feared that placing U.S. expats into senior roles on-site in Tokyo would hurt our ability to understand and leverage the very different Japanese culture. This could have impeded the dynamics with local senior management teams at an extremely critical time.

Our solution was to insert a shadow U.S. management team alongside local senior leadership. We kept the incumbent Japanese CEO, but had an American expat CEO as his peer. Similarly with the CFO, chief legal counsel, CIO, and so on, we maintained two roles with dual reporting. The theory was that the local people could focus on culture and dealing with issues in-country, and that the U.S. expats could provide the connectivity with the global headquarters that was needed to be effective. In any major acquisition like this, many elements of the business had to be coordinated with the head office. Whether it was access to capital, major new initiatives, legal issues, or compliance, an almost constant dialogue was required to deal with these day-to-day topics. We believed that the expat management team had built solid relationships with corporate employees over the years and could facilitate this most effectively.

As you might imagine, this strategy, which sounded so logical at the outset, ended up failing miserably. Having a U.S. CEO dialogue with a Japanese CEO when neither spoke the same language was the first issue. It was very hard to build a trusting relationship through an interpreter. Second, the solid connections between the U.S. CEO and the corporate office caused an air of distrust with the Japanese CEO, who had never even visited the U.S. headquarters. Both the Japanese and the Americans established their own cliques with communication among themselves, but not across the group. This led to a lack of trust and ultimately a failed platform.

A better approach, and one we ultimately migrated to, was to trust the local management team whom we had decided to back. We needed to give them the support and financial resources to be successful and empower them to do what they did best—run the business on a day-to-day basis. In this case, the importance of culture outweighed any advantages introduced by having the business managed out of a central location in the United States. Several local management members needed to be changed out over time, but on each occasion we were able to find a qualified local candidate to take their place. In fact, by giving the local team the authority they needed, but with support from the parent, we became one of the preferred employers in-country, allowing us to attract better and better talent.

But some level of oversight is still required in any cross-border deal. Liability for the entire company, including the Japanese subsidiary, remained with the U.S. CEO. The CEO and CFO both had a fiduciary, and personal, obligation to ensure compliance with laws and regulations before they signed off on the financial accounts. Once again, the cultural differences could complicate this. Often the regulations surrounding health and safety or the environment in these faraway countries might be less stringent than those in the United States.

So the question frequently arose, should we hold the foreign subsidiaries we acquired to the standard of care required in the United States or that of the local laws and customs? If we tried to impose U.S. regulations on these subsidiaries, we might make them less competitive locally. For example, complying with higher standards around the environment or health and safety might add costs that other local players did not have to incur. Or perhaps we had to pass on environmentally sensitive businesses or projects that our local competition was more than willing to take. Some would argue that we should let these subsidiaries play by the rules of the game in their country.

However, in the companies I worked for, we migrated to what I believe was the right answer. We would always defer to complying with the *most* stringent standards. If the U.S. standards were tighter, we enforced compliance there. If the local country regulations were more severe, that is the level of care we required. This was the only way to protect our company from lawsuits in either jurisdiction. We made sure to factor in this incremental cost of compliance to the financial projections of any cross-border deal we did. Failing to consider the impact or as importantly the cost of compliance with different regulations in different cultures can dramatically impact the financial results you achieve.

A SUMMARY OF OTHER BEST PRACTICES

Leadership and motivating people are critical elements of acquisition integration. What matters in certain cultures or age groups, for example, fancy titles, status, and pay levels, might be less important to others who are more interested in flexible work hours, interesting job content, or quality of life. Having an appreciation for these differences of opinion is a key to fostering the culture you are trying to set for your company.

I firmly believe that setting a culture that values diversity is essential to building a healthy organization. Left unguarded, people tend to surround themselves with others like themselves. It is human nature. You are generally more comfortable with people you have known for a long time, those who have the same values, interests, and experiences. Discussions tend to flow more easily than the awkwardness you often feel when meeting someone for the first time.

I have been fortunate enough to teach courses in M&A at several international schools, including Yale, Oxford, and Cambridge universities. For one to two years, MBA students have an incredible opportunity to be surrounded by and learn from smart people from different cultures with a wide variety of perspectives. Each semester, I assign a capstone project where students are allowed to pick their own groups. While there are always exceptions, the composition of these groups never ceases to amaze me. There is generally the North American group of American or Canadian students. There is the Asia group, or many times even a group comprised of Chinese students and another of Japanese. There is the Southeast Asia group from India and surrounding countries, a European group, an African group, and so forth.

What is happening here? Is it random? No; it is perfectly logical that students form groups with the people they know best, with similar experiences and outlooks. Why take a chance and form a group with people you don't know and who may end up being difficult? We have all been in that group at some point in our career with the member who does not do his or her fair share of the work and the rest of the group has to pick up the slack. It is much safer to stick with people you know and are most comfortable with.

My point is not to be overly critical of these students. In fact, despite all of my international assignments, my closest friends to this day are seven guys from North Haven, Connecticut, where I grew up 40 years ago. We only get together occasionally, but when we do, we immediately reconnect as a group due to our common experiences. It is like we never left; we are immediately comfortable with each other's presence. So I am certainly not in a position to preach as I still have friends in my comfort zone. Rather, my point is that you have to consider the opportunities that can be generated by forcing yourself out of your comfort zone to get different perspectives.

Allowing for a variety of opinions normally leads to better decision making. At one of my CEO roles, 50 percent of the management team were women and 30 percent were from outside the United States. I absolutely hired the best candidates for each job, but was fortunate to find a diverse group to do it. I do have to admit that the discussions were longer and at times frustrating because people did not always agree. In fact, most times they didn't. But having a variety of values, perspectives, and cultures sitting around the table ensured that we completed a better assessment of all options. It wasn't just my view as CEO that mattered; we were able to generate a much more complete view of the pros and cons of each issue.

But, equally important was that at the conclusion of the meeting, as CEO, I made a firm decision after taking input from the group. I needed to be clear that the debate was over. People had the chance to express their views, but now we needed to move on and implement. How many meetings have you been in where the debate continues to permeate even after the leader has supposedly made a decision? This can be very inefficient and delay the implementation of critical projects. Further, it can end up in allowing people who might not be right but who lobbied the hardest to get their way.

This again gets back to the culture you want to establish. In many Eastern cultures, there is the concept of "saving face." Participants in a meeting are very careful to not offend others publicly. It is viewed as rude and inappropriate. There tends to be at least the appearance of consensus around views, but the ultimate decision is made outside of the room.

As you move toward the West, most cultures tend to be more direct. As an American, it was important to me that I heard everyone out, but then made a firm decision that everyone followed. For you American readers, how many meetings have you been in where there is a major issue that people are afraid to bring up? What happens at the end of the meeting? Everyone goes back to their office and talks about the issue that should have come up in the meeting. My focus was to respect people's opinion, encourage them to express it, make a formal decision, and then move forward. While this seemed to work well for me over the years, it would clearly not be as effective in the more consensus-driven cultures of the West.

I can remember one of my first meetings when I moved from the United States to London. It was a presentation of an investment for approval and I sat on the firm's investment committee. On page two of the PowerPoint presentation I interrupted the speaker and asked a question. The entire group looked at me like I was crazy. I was used to the American rapid-fire questioning approach. When I brought deals to the General Electric Capital board, I rarely got past page three of the presentation and almost never had the time to go through every page.

But in my new environment, the protocol was to wait for the deal team to review the entire presentation, summarize your questions, and ask them at the completion of the talk. While this seemed very polite, I would argue that the best approach is somewhere between the two. In any event, this is a good example of how differences in culture can impact your approach.

It is the ability to set a culture that encourages and values diversity in the company that you buy that is important, in essence creating an environment at the newly acquired company that allows diversity to foster. I have worked with multiple companies over the years, but General Electric stands out as the one that best valued diversity in the workplace during my time there. Whether it was the "Women's Forum," the "African-American Forum," or employees from the LGBTQ community, GE had a way to make all employees feel valued and important. GE facilitated this by a variety of forums targeted at each group. There were local and regional meetings with active, and I stress *active*, participation by GE senior management. This was a great forum for employees to learn more about how GE views diversity and to offer suggestions on how to improve the culture. Alternately, it gave GE senior management the opportunity to evaluate talent, meet with individual employees, and help with the succession planning process.

Offering flexible working hours, working remotely from home, and on-site day care were all things that GE experimented with. For example, providing working mothers with more of a chance to be successful sent a message that GE valued diversity and was taking tangible steps to help progress it. As a result of these initiatives, diversity of the senior management team at GE improved over time, further reinforcing the process.

In an M&A context, the reporting structure you pick for a company post-acquisition sets one of the first tangible examples of the culture you are trying to establish. The first hundred days after any purchase is the most critical time. Target employees are concerned about everything from their jobs to their pay, to benefits, to the company location. It is a fine balance between trying to announce something immediately to quell people's fears versus waiting long enough to have a good understanding of the issues before committing to a course of action. Too many times snap decisions are made that later need to be reversed. This can impact the trust the target has in his or her new ownership.

To give one simple example, I was once placed in charge of integrating a newly acquired financial services company into the corporate parent. The two immediate issues I had to face still amaze me to this day. The first I was somewhat sympathetic to. It involved the appropriate job titles for our newly combined salesforce. At the acquired company, the more senior salespeople had the title of "Vice President." Alternatively, all salespeople at my company were called "Associates." This created a bit of a problem where peers in the newly combined organization now had different titles.

I have never been overly concerned with titles during my career, but the salespeople convinced me that it mattered in this situation. With a VP title, customers would view them as more empowered to deliver what they promised. In other words, they were senior enough to speak for the company without having to go to higher levels for approval. Having the VP title helped them get their foot in the door to make their sales pitch. This argument made sense to me and we eventually allowed salespeople to include the Vice President title on their business cards once they reached a tenure of three years with the company—problem solved.

The second issue was much less reasonable. I was in my office one Friday afternoon when one of the most senior salespeople from the acquired company entered my office. Not only was he the most senior, he was by far the most productive of the entire team, generating over $1 million of revenue per year. He said, "We have a problem." That afternoon he counted the number of ceiling tiles in his office. He counted *five* tiles long by ten tiles wide. He then went to the office of a more junior salesperson next to him and counted *six* tiles long by ten tiles wide and was actually upset that his office was smaller than a more junior salesperson. What does this say about how this very productive salesperson would fit into the egalitarian culture I was trying to build?

More importantly, what would it have said about the culture if I had acquiesced and given him a bigger office? This is an area where ethics and accountability interface with culture. In all honesty, it was a bit harder to tell my most productive salesperson that he would have to stay in a smaller office than it would have been if it was my least productive person. I ran the risk of losing a very talented and productive employee to a competitor as he was eminently marketable. But if his office size really mattered that much to him, I was better off without him on my team. Setting tangible examples of the culture you want to drive in an organization is essential to success.

Culture can be driven by things as simple as the layout of your office. In one role I suggested to my executive committee that we move to an open floor plan with no offices. I felt that this would enhance the flow of communication and deliver a more productive work environment. The reaction from most of my leadership team was overwhelmingly negative. How would we have confidential meetings? What if we now had to send sensitive data to centralized printers? What about the noise level? I heard dozens of reasons as to why an open floor plan, which worked so well for many other companies, would simply not be right for us. So I had to take the approach I mentioned earlier. I listened to the debate for a while, and then made a firm decision. However, even with this "firm" decision, I had several people continue to lobby me that they needed their own printer or had to have an office because they were different.

After weeks of debate, we finally had the floor plan laid out and it was time to select where we would sit. Again, I wanted to set a sense that all people were valued equally. I asked that my sitting area be in an internal space, with no windows. Sure enough when the seating plans came out a week later, my area was in the corner with bright windows and a fancy coffee machine right there. It took me several tries to convince the team that I really did want interior space right next to the rest rooms. Why was I taking all of this effort on an issue that seemed mundane? To set a tangible example to the organization of the culture I was trying to build at this company.

The formal structure and reporting lines of an organization can also be used to drive the desired culture. Two main approaches are the centralized and the decentralized approach. In a decentralized model, the target company is left mostly unchanged after it is purchased. Management generally have the same approval levels and authority to make decisions as they had on a stand-alone basis. There is little, if any, interaction with the remainder of the parent company's divisions or subsidiaries, at least at the start. In essence, the target company is treated as a stand-alone organization with its own culture and structure, largely as if nothing changed.

There are multiple benefits to a decentralized approach. First, and probably most importantly, it can drive a culture of autonomy, trust, and accountability. By letting the target company continue essentially as is, the buyer signals their confidence in the management team to keep growing the organization just as they had for many years prior to the acquisition. It is a big vote of confidence. Further, it mitigates the time normally required to adjust to a new owner, rebrand the target company, and adopt new policies and procedures, allowing the target to remain focused on customers and drive their business forward.

In a centralized approach, the target company is immediately consolidated into the operations of the buyer. They may be considered a separate division of a broader company or they may even cease to be a standalone reporting entity. Normally the approval and level of autonomy under a centralized approach are more limited than what management enjoyed as a stand-alone company. They are rebranded to become part of the new parent. Their company name and logo are usually changed. There is heavy interaction with corporate headquarters and, in most cases, sister divisions of the company. In other words, the target goes from being an autonomous unit to one piece of a much larger puzzle.

Advantages to this approach include commonality of practices, driving synergies, and in most cases lower costs. For example, a merger of the target into the parent frequently allows for a reduction in roles such as chief legal counsel, CFO, CIO, or even the CEO in some instances. The spans of controls of the headquarter roles can be expanded to include the target operations rather than having separate people in each division. Cost synergies can be delivered by streamlining operations and by things as simple as leveraging the purchasing power advantages of the larger parent company.

On the revenue side, a centralized approach facilitates the sharing of customer lists and cross-selling of products needed to drive the revenue improvements that may have been fundamental assumptions of the deal. By frequent interaction with the CEOs and sales teams of peer divisions of the conglomerate, the businesses can share best practices and help each other grow in adjacent markets with little incremental cost. This is very difficult in a decentralized approach where there is very little communication between operating units and each business has its own monthly operating metrics it has to achieve. In other words, if I have my own financial budget that I will be held to, why would I spend much time driving synergies for the overall organization that get recorded elsewhere? Good CEOs will continue to drive synergies for the benefit of the overall organization, but those struggling with their own businesses may not.

However, a centralized process if not managed properly can have very adverse impacts. Buyers have to remember that good acquisitions are done for a reason. Whether it was access to technology or entrance into new markets or products, there was something unique to buy that the parent did not already have. I have seen too many cases where an overdone centralized approach results in changing the target company from what was purchased into a clone of the parent company. If too many policies, procedures, rebranding, and culture elements are forced onto the acquired company over the years, it can ultimately revert back to looking just like the parent. There needs to be a balance between standardization and delivering synergies while doing the right level of integration to maximize the value of what was just bought.

A second issue with the centralized approach is the potential impact on management. Going for a completely autonomous business to a division of a larger company with new policies and approval levels can be a significant adjustment for the target management team. Handled properly it can work, but the first tendency for the new management may be to resist the heightened level of supervision. They are used to running their own show and making decisions on their own. Now they have to ask others for permission. While driving a culture is easier when operations are centralized, for similar reasons the target may resist this approach.

Finally, it can become very hard to track the results of the acquisition versus what was forecast when the target company is fully consolidated into the parent. Even if kept as a separate division, the consolidation of financial results and intercompany transactions can skew the view of operating performance of what you actually bought. This makes it very hard, if not impossible, to return to the deal a year later and compare what was forecast at the board to get the deal approved to the ultimate results achieved.

The life-cycle of a business is another area that can materially impact a culture and may need to change over time. You often see this when a family-run business is purchased by private equity with plans to aggressively grow the company and then take it public. Think about the characteristics needed to grow a company from an idea on paper to a successful business that has survived for years. You need a CEO who is innovative and willing to take risks. You need someone who has deep domain expertise and good relationships with customers. This person, particularly in a family-run business, generally surrounds herself with trusted longtime advisors in the CFO, chief legal counsel, and other key roles. In many cases, the CFO of a smaller family-run company is more of an accountant who keeps the books, prepares tax returns, and does financial planning.

Compare this to the skill set needed to run a Fortune 500 company. This CEO may need to be a bit more risk averse given the diversity of shareholders she needs to respond to, the regulatory pressures, the complexity of the business, and sheer demands on her time. She will have staff to help her innovate and deliver the next key products to customers rather than spending her time to do it herself. The company's CFO will likely be more of a strategic partner with a broad business perspective rather than an accountant. The finance function will include an army of tax accountants, financial planners, and certified public accountants to help manage the finance function.

In summary, the role of the CEO, CFO, and other senior management in a Fortune 500 company is more of an emissary to the different stakeholder groups. They are focused on getting the best teams possible, stakeholder management, strategy, and governance. This could not be more different than the tensions facing a CEO of a family-run business. Day-to-day management, access to capital, customer relations, monthly budgeting, staffing needs, and the delivery of products and services make up most of the day for a family-owned CEO.

While the two ends of the spectrum from family-run CEO to Fortune 500 CEO are clearly distinguishable, the evolution between the two can be extraordinarily difficult. In many cases, a tension can arise between the family CEO and the new private equity owners. While some people do have both, the skillset to get the family-run business to a certain size changes when a company is considering an IPO. It becomes much more about strategy, putting on a good roadshow for sophisticated investors, and at times making tough decisions about the next steps for the business. It also becomes quite hard to sustain the culture that was required to get the company to where it needed to be, but to still work as a public company. Alternately, many Fortune 500 companies struggle with how to maintain an innovative and streamlined approach when they have become complex and global players. The best companies are able to find the right balance between the two. But knowing what you are good at and, more importantly, what you are not is a critical element of success.

So what are the conclusions with respect to the importance of culture for mergers and acquisitions?

1. Setting the right culture is absolutely critical to any business and especially so when buying a new company.
2. Failure to adequately assess the impact culture in a target company is one of the most frequent reasons cited for acquisition failure.
3. Culture is a soft concept that is very difficult to define, implement, and manage. There are no hard-and-fast rules on what culture is best or the pragmatic steps to implement it. It really depends on the situation at hand and the long-term goals of the company.
4. Being sensitive and aware that different cultures exist, not only in cross-border deals but within domestic companies, is an important first step.
5. Setting the right culture is largely about leadership, personal accountability, setting tangible examples, and making tough choices.
6. The type of organization structure you choose, centralized versus decentralized, can help facilitate how you want to imbed a culture in a company you just purchased. Either approach, implemented properly, can help you drive the desired results.

7. Try to force yourself out of your comfort zone and interact with different types of people. This will stimulate learning in both a professional and personal environment and help you make more informed decisions.
8. Be especially careful in cross-border deals with respect to cultural differences. Make sure you have people on the ground in the countries you invest in to help understand the culture, business environment, and practices.

What we have learned over time is that an attention to culture, various constituencies and effective leadership can make the difference between a successful acquisition and a failed one.

CHAPTER 6

Who Is Behind the Curtain?

Government is not the solution to the problem, government is the problem.

—Ronald Reagan

A CASE STUDY: LLOYDS HBOS

HBOS, a large financial services conglomerate, was one of the most respected banks in the world. It was the largest retail mortgage provider in the U.K. with a market share of 20 percent and balances of approximately $400 billion. On September 17, 2008, several days after the bankruptcy filing of Lehman Brothers, HBOS's share price experienced enormous volatility, reaching a high of 220p and falling to a low of 88p. Over the next three days, share prices plunged 37 percent amid fears of an impending collapse. HBOS voiced concern that depositors and lenders had started withdrawing from the bank, prompting a run-on-the-bank type of situation.

Fearing that the failure of the country's largest mortgage lender would have catastrophic repercussions on the U.K. financial system, the U.K. government arranged a merger between HBOS and Lloyds TSB. The government pushed the acquisition by promising to override competitive laws using a national interest clause to maintain the "stability of financial system." Gordon Brown, then prime minister of the U.K., became personally involved to ensure that the deal was successful.

After intense negotiations lasting less than 48 hours, Lloyds TSB and HBOS announced the terms of the transaction on September 18, 2008, valuing HBOS at $20 billion. Eric Daniels, then chief executive of Lloyds, admitted that Lloyds and HBOS had been in touch about possible deals since 2001 but were always discouraged by stringent competition laws and issues, which had suddenly been relaxed by the government now that the economy was in crisis mode.

One might question how the team from Lloyds was able to analyze a complex financial institution with balances of over $400 billion in a matter of two days. How did they go about evaluating management? How extensive a review of legal contracts, financial results, budgets, board minutes, and so on could be done in the span of 48 hours? Further, why were the stringent completion laws that had prevented a merger from happening for over a year suddenly no longer a problem?

Sure enough, on October 13, 2008, the terms of the acquisition were revised downwards following the announcement of the government's $60 billion capital investment support for banks and the subsequent fall in

HBOS's share price. The revised terms valued HBOS at $10 billion, half of the original anticipated value.

Although the Lloyds HBOS merger gave momentary relief to HBOS, it compromised Lloyds TSB both in the short term and the long term. The strategy of merging Lloyds with HBOS was counter to the "separation of the good bank from the bad bank" strategy followed by other financial institutions. Many banking institutions would follow a strategy of separating their assets into two vehicles. Assets they no longer want to pursue, like subprime mortgages or complex derivatives, were put into a "bad bank" and were either wound down over time or offered for sale to private equity firms, other banks, and distressed-asset buyers at heavily discounted prices.

Assets that the bank wanted to continue marketing, such as corporate loans, debt instruments, equity capital markets, and so forth, were put into the "good bank" and continued to be supported. The argument was that management could now focus on parts of the business they wanted to continue and that, even at heavily discounted prices, it was worth getting rid of the "bad" assets to limit further exposure and potential distraction to the management team.

But given the extremely short time frame Lloyds had to make a decision, management did not sift through the HBOS assets for only the ones they wanted; they had to buy everything. Many of these assets proved to be more impaired than even HBOS itself believed. Lloyds' overpayment for the assets and the continued distraction to the management team drove a decline in results of the newly merged entity. As a result, the government had to eventually step in again, this time with taxpayers' money, to strengthen the balance sheet of the merged entity, resulting in the taxpayers owning 43.5 percent of Lloyds HBOS. The merged entity was subsequently renamed Lloyds Banking Group (LBG). Unfortunately, despite the government's help, Lloyds has never really recovered from this failed acquisition.

Whether the goal is to save the economy, protect depositors, regulate executive compensation, or for nationalistic concerns, there is an increasing trend toward government involvement in M&A transactions globally. In some cases, the results of government intervention have been justified. In others, the involvement of the government just makes matters worse, often resulting in billions of dollars of incremental cost to taxpayers. A deeper analysis of the Lloyds HBOS transaction helps to illustrate the pros and cons of government intervention into mergers and acquisitions.

HBOS History

HBOS was formed through the merger of Halifax and the Bank of Scotland in 2001, a diversified financial services group engaged in banking, insurance brokering, and financial services throughout the U.K. and internationally. Just prior to the start of the Great Recession, HBOS was the largest retail mortgage provider in the U.K. with a market share of 20 percent and balances of approximately $400 billion. HBOS was also the largest liquid savings provider in the U.K. with a market share of 15 percent. For the financial year ended December 31, 2007, HBOS reported revenues of $34 billion and generated profit before tax of $9.0 billion. A significant portion of HBOS's portfolio was comprised of commercial property lending.

Twenty-eight percent of HBOS's mortgage book was in the riskier, higher-margin specialist areas, principally buy-to-rent and self-certified loans. No background checks were performed in a self-certified loan; the information submitted by the applicant was taken at face value without being verified. In the United States, these loans were called "liar loans" because mortgage applicants frequently exaggerated their financial condition to obtain more financing than they could ultimately pay back. Nevertheless, HBOS continued to aggressively expand its mortgage book long after other players had stopped doing so. This was all fine until the housing market collapsed.

By the start of 2008, U.K. house prices had already fallen by 12 percent, the largest decline since 1983. Analysts were estimating a further drop of 15–20 percent in 2008–2009, but the house-price-to-income ratio, a key indicator of affordability, suggested that house prices would fall even more. This dramatic downturn in the housing market started to reveal broad issues with HBOS. HBOS was a sales-oriented bank with poor risk management at times. Paul Moore, head of regulatory risk at HBOS during 2002–2004, said, "I think a concern everybody had was whether or not the business was under control."

The liability side of the HBOS balance sheet complicated things significantly. HBOS relied on wholesale financing to sustain operations. In other words, HBOS did not have significant customer deposits to fund its business. Rather it was dependent on raising money through loans from other banks or the capital markets via issuance of public debt or equity. When the capital markets dried up with the financial crisis, HBOS's access to financing dried up as well. A $315 billion mismatch between customer deposits the bank had on hand and the amount of money it had lent to others made the bank dangerously reliant on the capital markets (i.e., the company had issued $315mm of loans in excess to the level of deposits it maintained and could no longer borrow to make up the difference).

The combination of HBOS's exposure to $45 billion in toxic assets, very aggressive mortgage lending practices, and a reliance on wholesale funding put severe pressure on the bank's stock price. With the credit crisis unfolding, HBOS's share price slid further. The cost of HBOS's credit default spreads,[1] an indication of the creditworthiness of the entity, continued to be higher than its peers, indicating that investors had lower faith in the company's viability as a going concern.

Lloyds History

Lloyds Bank combined with Trustee Savings Banks (TSB) to form Lloyds TSB in 1995. After a period of turmoil, the bank began a new, customer-centric strategy under Eric Daniel's leadership that involved sale of a number of non-core assets and a strict U.K. geographic focus. The group was organized into three main divisions: U.K. Retail & Mortgages, Wholesale & International Banking, and Insurance & Investment. This made the bank one of the largest mortgage lenders in the U.K.

Over the years, Lloyds transformed its business model into a more conservative and conventional bank. Unlike HBOS, Lloyds had successfully avoided relying on wholesale funding to grow its assets; it had ample customer deposits on hand to fund the business. The bank had strict risk management processes in place and focused on cross-selling different products to its customers. A large part of this transformation was credited to management. Investors actually saw this stock as a defensive bet, providing stable earnings in times of uncertainty. Lloyds had a distinctive advantage over its peers as it had an AAA debt rating and was not reliant on wholesale funding to stay alive, even in a financial crisis.

Merger Timeline

The series of events leading to a full government bailout of HBOS and the public's reaction clearly illustrate the pros and cons of active involvement in M&A by government bodies:

- *Early 2008:* The housing market in the U.K., the United States, and other developed economies came under severe stress with housing prices falling and credit supply virtually drying up. A crisis of confidence took down Bear-Stearns in March 2008, requiring an intervention by the U.S. government. Rumors of HBOS's funding problems resulted in a 17 percent drop in share price. With $400 billion in customer deposits a run on HBOS would have risked the entire U.K. financial system.

    The Financial Services Authority (FSA) and Bank of England came out with strong statements in support of HBOS, which comforted the market and HBOS's shares gained back some of the losses. However, an attempt by HBOS to raise new equity was less than successful due to continuing concerns about exposure to the property market. With the collapse of Lehman in September 2008, the focus turned to HBOS's exposure to the property market and its wholesale funding model. With the seizing up of the credit markets, panicked investors started dumping HBOS stocks, creating a run-on-the-bank type of situation.

- *September 17, 2008:* It was reported by the *Independent* that "Britain's largest mortgage bank cannot and will not be allowed to fail" due to having "some $400 billion in retail deposits." Speculation about a possible merger began. The *Financial Times* reported that on the night of September 17, 2008, the government had "brokered a deal to save the country's largest mortgage lender from a crisis of confidence" and said that Lloyds had been the only lender willing to take on HBOS without a large government guarantee.

- *September 18, 2008:* Lloyds TSB makes an acquisition offer to HBOS shareholders. The key elements of the announcement were:
  - HBOS shareholders were offered 0.83 Lloyds TSB share per HBOS share held, amounting to $3.7 per share value at the previous night's close, valuing the business at $19 billion and giving HBOS shareholders 44 percent of the enlarged group. The offer value of $3.7 per share was a 60 percent premium to previous day's closing price. Lloyds TSB chairman Victor Blank and CEO Eric Daniels would lead the combined bank and HBOS CEO Andy Hornby would stay with the group.
  - The U.K. government circumvented Competition Commission intervention to get the transaction approved. The combined bank would now control 28 percent of the residential mortgage market and 33 percent of the market in personal current accounts. Lloyds TSB/HBOS would also rank first in U.K. retail savings, personal loans and credit cards, household insurance, and bank assurance and hold a top-three position in commercial banking and mid-corporate banking. Pressure to get the deal done, in fact to get *any* deal done, influenced the government to overlook any competitive issues associated with the large market share the combined company would now have.

- *September 19, 2008:* HBOS shares close at $1.95 per share, well below the $3.71 price offered by Lloyds. Stock analysts speculate that the deal must be off.

- *October 1, 2008:* Scottish politician Margo Macdonald called for an investigation after reading Lloyds TSB and HBOS chairmen's "joyous comments" following a takeover, which she pointed out was "unimpeded by the usual rules governing such big business deals." She said Prime Minister Gordon Brown and Chancellor of Exchequer Alistair Darling were wrong to waive the normal referral to the Competition Commission, and that the FSA had been "curiously quiet."

Brown reiterates his support for the deal, which reassured some that the merger might happen. Support from institutional investors in the stock, in part driven by discussions from Gordon Brown and Chancellor Alistair Darling, pushed HBOS shares up 21 percent to $2.36 while Lloyds TSB ended 10 percent higher at $4.50. Bank of England also extended its "lender of last resort" facility to HBOS in a secret deal that was not disclosed to the public, including to the shareholders of Lloyds, until a year after.

- *October 7, 2008:* Darling and his team scrambled to put together a bailout package for the retail banking industry, as it became clear that not just HBOS, but all of the major banks were now suffering in the market. Banking stocks had opened with huge sell orders and no bids, sending shares into freefall. RBS had plunged 40 percent and others were declining as well. The bailout package included ~£50bn in capital injections to the banks, extension of the existing liquidity scheme, and £250bn in government guaranteed funding.

That evening the Treasury called the banks in to discuss the bailout package. Mr. Daniels was impressive, according to insiders, grasping the concept quickly and pointing out issues that had been overlooked. He insisted that Lloyds did not need money, although he accepted that HBOS, which had agreed to a rescue takeover on September 17, did in fact require help.

- *October 10, 2008:* The government announces a $60 billion capital investment support package for the banks.[2]
- *October 11, 2008:* Banks are called again for meetings with the Treasury to discuss final details of the capital injection. Mr. Daniels was surprised to learn that the Treasury believed that Lloyds and HBOS needed £17 billion. The Treasury warned that should Mr. Daniels be tempted to walk away from the deal, Lloyds alone would have to take an $11.2 billion charge if they did not go through with the merger. Lloyds saw the move as the government's way to put on pressure so it did not abandon the HBOS deal.
- *October 13, 2008:*[3] Further deterioration in the financial markets saw HBOS's share price fall to $1.44, representing a drop of 28 percent over previous close price. Lloyds revised terms of the acquisition to 0.605 Lloyds share for every share of HBOS. The revised offer valued HBOS at approximately $9.9 billion. Lloyds and HBOS also planned to raise $27 billion under a government-funded recapitalization program to further stabilize the bank's funding position.

Commenting on the developments, Sir Victor Blank, chairman of Lloyds TSB, said, "Today's news is good for investors and customers alike. Lloyds TSB's already robust financial position is further enhanced by today's capital raising, which in turn allows us to drive forward with our plans to acquire HBOS. Our trading update underlines that our core business is strong and growing. Our customers can feel confident that their money is secure. Lloyds TSB is and remains a great place to bank."

■ *October 31, 2008:*[4] A formal approval of the Lloyds HBOS takeover was granted by the government, waiving U.K. competition rules. The Office of Fair Trading (OFT), in a report published on October 24, 2008 (Office of Fair Trading, 2008), had raised concerns that the proposed merger between Lloyds and HBOS would lead to significant lessening of competition.

Peter Mandelson, Secretary of State for Business, empowered by a Parliamentary approval of "the stability of the U.K. financial system" consideration in the Enterprise Act of 2002, decided not to refer the Lloyds HBOS merger to the Competition Commission. Mr. Mandelson said, "I am satisfied that on balance the public interest is best served by allowing this merger to proceed without a reference to the Competition Commission." On October 24, the Parliament added the "Stability of the Financial System" as a consideration of "public interest" as to whether deals should be allowed to happen. It appears that the government put the stability of the U.K. financial system ahead of any concerns about the anticompetitive nature of two large banks combining.

■ *November 19, 2008:* More than 96 percent of Lloyds' shareholders approved the takeover of HBOS and fundraising plans.

■ *December 1, 2008:* A group of Scottish consumers filed a complaint to the Competition Appeal Tribunal on December 1, 2008, against the merger. The complaint was rejected after a very quick hearing.

■ *December 12, 2008:*[5] The investors of HBOS voted in favor of a takeover by Lloyds. The share prices of both HBOS and Lloyds reacted negatively, with HBOS closing down 20 percent and Lloyds falling 17 percent.

■ *January 12, 2008:*[6] Final legal approval of the merger was granted by a court in Edinburgh, leading to the formal creation of a super-bank. The Treasury ended up owning 43.4 percent of the merged bank as only .24 percent of the newly issued shares offered to shareholders of HBOS were purchased. At Lloyds this number was only .5 percent.

What went wrong here? Did the government have the right to waive any concerns over the impact to bank competition by such a large merger? Were they right to intervene and influence the Lloyds management team to go ahead with the deal? Given the long-term implications to Lloyds and the U.K. banking system, one could argue whether the impact of government intervention was effective. In other words, would the Lloyds HBOS merger have worked out better, or not even happened at all, if the government got involved? Should the government have exerted its influence to allow a transaction that, left to its own devices, would likely never have been done?

This is an interesting question that could be argued either way. As in most cases where the government does decide to get involved in a global acquisition, the argument in favor of this involvement was that country's economic stability was dependent on both parties to the transaction continuing to be viable. In this case, with one of the parties to the merger in serious financial difficultly, the combination of the two would hopefully result in one larger, stronger entity with more market share. In other words, if the distressed party were allowed fail, the effects would ripple through the economy and have a much broader impact than simply the failure of one bank.

This could well have been true in the case of Lloyds HBOS Since HBOS was bailed out by Lloyds and the government, we will never know what would have happened to the U.K. or even the global economy had this support not been provided. The merger may well have prevented significant deterioration in market stability. However, there are several material consequences with a strategy such as was employed here.

Moral Hazard

The concept of moral hazard is that institutions and their management teams will increase their level of risk-taking behavior if they know that their downside is protected. Think about an example of going to a casino. What if you knew that if you lost money, someone was going to reimburse you for 100 percent of this loss, that is, if you gambled and won, you kept the money, but if you lost money, you would be fully reimbursed? Would you be as cautious with your money? The concept of moral hazard argues that people will take increasing levels of risk if their downside is protected. Why not try to make the most money possible in the time you have by taking the largest bets you can when you have no downside risk?

In the corporate world, banks might follow the same behavior if they knew the government would always come in to bail them out. Why not enter into aggressive mortgage securities or complex derivatives if there was no risk to you if they went bad? As the government bailed out more and more banks, this temptation would get worse and worse. Some would argue that the government should have allowed HBOS to fail in order to stop this cycle of moral hazard from getting worse. It would have made management teams realize that they had to accept the consequences of their decisions.

Confusion to Stakeholders

CEOs of large corporations have multiple constituencies to serve. First and foremost, shareholders have entrusted their money to the company management by using their own cash to buy stock. The CEO and management team have a responsibility to use this capital as judiciously as possible and someday return it, plus a premium to shareholders. One could argue that while Lloyds' bailout of HBOS may have saved the British economy, it was not in the long-term interest of its shareholders given what happened to the company's share price after the merger was completed.

Employees are another critical constituency. Each company employee has a family that is likely dependent on the pay and benefits they receive by working at the corporation. CEOs have a responsibility to treat employees fairly and be prudent in making a solid, financially strong company.

Finally, one could argue that companies have a broader responsibility to the environment and local communities they serve. Increasingly corporate and social responsibility is becoming a critical element of a company's strategy. People are demanding that companies take a responsible approach to the environment and the broader economy.

So let's evaluate Lloyds' decision to buy HBOS in this context. As noted earlier, the deal perhaps saved a dramatic downturn in the economy if HBOS had failed. There was clearly some short-term turmoil, but there was never a run on the bank where depositors demanded their money back. By improving the overall economy, Eric Daniels arguably improved the environment Lloyds was able to continue operating in.

It is a bit harder to argue that this deal was a positive for employees and shareholders of the bank. The stock price of Lloyds was surely impacted by the decision to move forward. Shareholders experienced a dramatic loss in wealth as a direct result. As the stock price declined, management had to cut cost through widespread employee layoffs, so many employees were negatively impacted as well. Taxpayer money was used to take a 43 percent stake by the government in the combined entity. Again, one could debate whether saving a failed bank was the best use of taxpayer money.

Short-Term versus Long-Term Focus

The U.K. government seemed to be motivated primarily by short-term concerns. A run on HBOS would have caused immediate and dramatic results to the financial system. The more strategic question was the expected impact in the medium to long term. Eric Daniels was quoted as saying:

> *We thought that the HBOS acquisition in the short term would be painful. It has turned out, given that the economy has trended down even further, to be a very true statement. But we also believe it is strategically a very good acquisition and will prove to be so in a couple of years.*[7]

Ability to Back Out

Daniels received significant pressure to carry on with the transaction even when it became apparent that HBOS performance and the state of the economy was worse than he had originally expected. It put him in a very difficult position. Was he primarily responsible for his employees and company or for saving the U.K. economy? This is a great example of how seemingly obvious deals can cause unexpected problems.

Political Instability

Finally, the efforts to avoid the U.K. compensation commission on this deal are surprising. This is what gave rise for Margo McDonald, a member of the Scottish National Party, to call for an investigation over the facts and circumstances of the proposed merger. It seems that in the rush to save the bank, some of the normal procedures around anti-competition were not strictly followed.

What we do know is that the deal has had a lasting, arguably negative impact on Lloyds. Still today a £350 million shareholder lawsuit ($450 million) is outstanding against Lloyds for the damage caused to the company by the HBOS purchase. The distraction to management time, financial losses, and punitive fees from this recent lawsuit show the dangers of completing a complicated deal with very little due diligence. As we see in this case, the financial impact and distraction to the management can last for years after the deal is completed.

A CASE STUDY: KRAFT BUYS CADBURY

Kraft's purchase of Cadbury is an example of the government and cultural tensions that often surround cross-border acquisitions. In cross-border deals, the interests of each country have to be considered in addition to the normal views around pricing, structure, and the strategic intent of the deal. An increasing sense of nationalism across the world has put pressure on governments to put their country's interests first rather than protecting the parties trying to do the deal. It is often these softer issues that determine whether the deal gets approved by regulatory bodies and whether the ultimate outcome of the transaction is successful, more than the hard facts around pricing, legal terms, and conditions.

Kraft History

Few companies in corporate America have as complicated a history as Kraft Foods, the owner of Oreo cookies, Ritz crackers, and Oscar Mayer lunch meats. The company has a long and complex story, using mergers and acquisitions as a primary means of growth:

- *1903:* James L. Kraft begins selling cheese from a horse-drawn wagon in Chicago. By 1914, his company begins manufacturing cheese on its own. Over the ensuing decades, Kraft starts or acquires brands including Vegemite, Philadelphia cream cheese, Tombstone pizza, and Kraft macaroni and cheese.
- *1980s:* Cigarette maker R.J. Reynolds merges with snack company Nabisco Brands, owner of brands such as Ritz and Oreo, to form RJR Nabisco. Then RJR Nabisco becomes the target of the most legendary corporate raid of all time. After a fierce bidding war engulfing some of the biggest Wall Street banks and investors in the world, buyout firm Kohlberg Kravis Roberts in 1988 wins a $25 billion takeover of RJR Nabisco.
- *2000:* Philip Morris adds Nabisco Holdings, which RJR Nabisco had just left as a separate company. The Nabisco purchase was eventually valued at around $19.2 billion. The cigarette giant then combines Nabisco with Kraft.
- *2001:* Philip Morris spins off a small portion of its stake in Kraft Foods, which becomes publicly traded. Kraft executive Irene Rosenfeld left to PepsiCo's Frito-Lay division, but returns to Kraft in 2006.
- *2007:* Altria Group (the renamed Philip Morris) completes a spinoff of its majority stake in Kraft. Under pressure from investor Nelson Peltz, Kraft also agrees to sell its Post line of cereal—Grape-Nuts, Honey Bunches of Oats, and more.
- *2010:* Kraft closes a roughly $19 billion purchase of U.K. candy company Cadbury after a lengthy fight. Kraft also sells its Digiorno frozen pizza line to Nestle. Warren Buffett, the largest shareholder of Kraft, called both transactions "dumb." Today, Buffett says he supports Kraft's decision to break up.[8]
- *2011:* Kraft announces its intention to split up into two publicly traded companies. This is a surprising development, coming just 18 months after its massive acquisition of Cadbury. Kraft said it had two classes of brands that could be best managed separately and also attract investors who want to bet either on the global growth aspirations of snacks or on the slower growing but steady grocery business in North America.

Its proposed global snacks business included Kraft's European business and developing markets units, as well as snacks and confectionary businesses in North America. With about $32 billion in estimated revenue, it included Oreo cookies, Cadbury chocolates, and Trident gum, all of which had greater prospects for growth in emerging markets and to sell more to consumers on the go. Maxwell House coffee and Jell-O snacks lacked the growth potential of these products but came with stronger margins and more reliable sales. The global snacks business has an estimated $16 billion in revenue.

Cadbury History

Cadbury was the venerable British institution started by John Cadbury, a Quaker businessman selling cocoa from his grocer's shop in 1824. The business passed down through the family until in 1905 Cadbury introduced the Dairy Milk Bar, which became its best-selling product in no time. Other products developed over the years included Whole Nut Bar, Flake, Crunchie, and Cream-filled Eggs. During WWI, Cadbury diversified to providing clothing, books, and chocolate to soldiers while 2,000 of Cadbury's employees joined the armed services themselves.

Modern-day Cadbury was formed by a merger with drinks company Schweppes in 1969. The combined business went on to acquire Sunkist, Canada Dry, and other major drink names. Snapple, Mistic, and Stuarts brands were sold by Triarc to Cadbury Schweppes in 2000 for $1.45 billion, with the purchase of Royal Crown later that year as well.

On May 2, 2008, Kraft and Cadbury were split back out into one unit for drinks and another focusing on confectionary and chocolates. In mid-2009 Cadbury replaced some of the cocoa butter in their non-U.K. chocolate products with palm oil. Despite stating this was a response to consumer demand to improve taste and texture, there was no "new, improved recipe" claim placed on New Zealand labels. Consumer backlash was significant from environmentalists and chocolate lovers. By August 2009, the company announced that it was reverting to the use of cocoa butter in New Zealand and would source cocoa beans through Fair Trade channels. As part of Kraft's purchase of Cadbury in 2010, they agreed to honor all of Cadbury's commitments with respect to social responsibility in this area.

Background to the Deal

The Cadbury board advised its shareholders to accept an offer of 840 pence a share—valuing the company at £11.5bn ($18.9bn). The offer consisted of 500 pence in cash, with the rest made up of Kraft shares. Kraft borrowed £7bn ($11.5bn) to finance the deal. Kraft said the deal would create a "global confectionery leader." But there are renewed fears over possible job cuts at Cadbury's U.K. operations as a result of the agreed takeover.

This offer was a significant increase on earlier Kraft bids, which were flatly turned down by the Cadbury board as "derisory." Kraft's previous offers valued the company at £10.5bn—a bid Cadbury's chairman, Roger Carr, said was an attempt to "buy Cadbury on the cheap." David Cumming, head of U.K. equities at Cadbury shareholder Standard Life, said that he would support the deal despite hoping for a higher price. "I won't go against the view of Cadbury's management," he told the BBC. "Kraft are getting a good deal. It's sad that Cadbury is gone, but business is business."

Worries About Job Cuts

Unions expressed concerns that the Kraft takeover could cost jobs. Kraft gave no specific assurances over the future of 4,500 U.K. jobs, though it said it would invest in the Bournville site and maintain production at the Somerdale plant. Kraft did not rule out cuts at Cadbury's head office in Uxbridge. Kraft said it expected "meaningful cost savings" as a result of the merger, but assured investors that Somerdale would remain open and they would try to mitigate employee layoffs throughout the business.

Jennie Formby from the Unite union said the need for Kraft to cut costs could mean staff reductions in the longer term. "We are concerned about the levels of debt that Kraft has," she told the BBC. "The sad truth is that when they have to pay down that debt, the soft option is jobs and conditions. When you have to make cost savings of the magnitude they will need to make, you have to ask where those cost savings will be made."

Those fears were shared by David Bailey, professor at Coventry University Business School. "Serious questions need to be asked about Kraft's intentions," he said. "Kraft already has a track record of cutting production and moving production abroad. There's no guarantee that they'll keep production in the U.K. in the long run."[9]

Worries About Corporate Social Responsibility

As a part of the deal, Kraft promised to honor Cadbury's existing fair-trade sourcing commitments in response to fears that a U.S. food company would stop selling ethically sourced products after the takeover. For example, Kraft promised to honor Cadbury's existing deal to sell fair-trade chocolate after fears that it would stop selling ethically sourced confectionery if its takeover went ahead.

Jonathan Horrell, the U.K. corporate affairs director for the U.S. food conglomerate, said Kraft already worked "extensively" with sustainably sourced cocoa and coffee suppliers and planned to maintain Cadbury's contracts with the Fairtrade Foundation. But he would not confirm whether Kraft would continue Cadbury's ongoing talks to expand its use of fair-trade cocoa beans into other brands—a major and continuing worry for the Fairtrade Foundation.

Horrell said, "We would expect to honor Cadbury's commitments to sustainable and ethical sourcing, including Fairtrade, if our offer moves forward, but it's premature to discuss any details at this stage." But Horrell said this was as far as Kraft would go, leaving a question mark over proposals to increase Cadbury's use of fair-trade produce. "That's where the 'premature' comment comes in," he said. "Because we don't actually own Cadbury at this stage, we need to understand more about all these things. As I said, we certainly expect to honour their commitments." The current deal to supply Cadbury with fair-trade cocoa beans from Ghana is understood to be time-limited, which also leaves it open to Kraft to end the tie-in when the existing contract ends.[10]

Market Response

The deal reshaped the global chocolate industry. It would now be dominated by just four large companies: Kraft/Cadbury, Mars, Nestle, and Ferrero. Nestle was put in the unusual position of being third place, behind Mars and the new Kraft/Cadbury giant, an unfamiliar role for the world's largest food corporation. As a result, Nestle began eyeing up Hershey, an American company with an iconic status similar to Cadbury in the U.K.[11]

Kraft's £11.9bn takeover of dairy milk maker Cadbury is a "bad deal," according to Warren Buffett, the billionaire investor who is the U.S. company's biggest shareholder. "I have a lot of doubts," Mr. Buffett said, adding that he would vote against the bid if he had the chance. Kraft's shares dropped in premarket trading after Mr. Buffett's comments.

Despite his criticism, Buffett rejected the suggestion that he show his displeasure by selling Berkshire's stake of over 9 percent in Kraft. That, he says, would be too expensive because Kraft's stock is still "undervalued" but not as undervalued as it was three weeks ago. Buffett also strongly criticized Kraft's recent sale of a pizza business to Nestle at a price he believed was too low. He indicated that "deal momentum" fueled by the investment bankers may have helped push the Kraft/Cadbury deal forward.[12]

So, despite all of these arguably legitimate concerns, the Kraft/Cadbury deal closed as scheduled. But it did have long-lasting impacts on the M&A industry. For example, more stringent views of antitrust regulations have continued to quell rumors as recent as June 2016 that Nestle would still like to buy Hershey. Deals in food and other industries are being increasingly scrutinized by regulators and turned down because the combination of such large firms in the same industry is viewed as reducing competition and thereby increasing prices paid by consumers.

Further, the inherent nationalism around foreign corporations buying treasured domestic companies with long histories continues to grow. The takeover of Cadbury caused the U.K. government to review and change how foreign firms could buy U.K. companies. The U.K. government began to feel that it was simply too easy for foreign firms to buy U.K. rivals and therefore started to build in legal protections.

The U.K. "Panel of Takeovers and Mergers" made changes to the laws in September 2011 to make this much harder, including:

- Demanding more information from bidders on their intentions after purchase. This was a particular issue in Kraft/Cadbury as Kraft management closed a local factory one week after closing the deal, despite making representations to the contrary before the deal closed.
- Target companies must now disclose not only that they have a potential buyer, but who it is and what are their intentions.
- Removal of "breakup fee." Prior to the rules change, bidders could request that the seller pay them a material fee, in some cases millions of dollars, for backing away from the transaction once agreement had been met. This made it very hard for sellers to walk away if things changed between signing and closing the contract. The removal of these fees vastly improved the power of a U.K. company being targeted in an acquisition.

So while many cross-border deals continue to get done, they are under much more scrutiny today. The overall polices regarding how much a government wants to get involved in the private sector, their positons on global trade, and the regulatory impact around acquisitions all have an impact on the number and nature of deals getting done. With the advent of the Trump Administration in the United States, it will be fascinating to see how the "hidden hand of government" will influence the global economy and the fallout impact on cross-border mergers and acquisitions.

NOTES

1. Credit Default Swaps (CDS) are a way for one party to get insurance on a decline in the creditworthiness of another company. If the company defaults on an obligation, the issuer of the CDS reimburses the credit losses of the person who bought it. The price of a CDS moves inversely to the creditworthiness of the related company, that is, the price for the insurance protection increases as the creditworthiness of the company declines.

2. http://www.parliament.uk/documents/commons/lib/research/rp 2008/rp08-777
   .pdf.
3. http://news.c.co.uk/1/hi/business/7666710.stm.
4. http://www.telegraph.co.uk/finance/recession/3287506/Lloyds-TSB-take-over-of
   -HBOS-to-be-rubberstamped.html.
5. http://business.timesonline.co.uk/tol/business/industry   sectors/banking   and
   finance/article5330783.ece.
6. http://news.bbc.co.uk/1/hi/business/7823521.sm.
7. "Banking Crisis, Dealing with the Failure of the UK Banks", House of Commons
   Treasury Committee, Seventh Report of Session, 2008-2009 Page 12.
8. http://blogs.wsj.com/deals/2011/08/04/the-long-strange-history-of-kraft-foods.
9. http://news.bbc.co.uk/2/hi/8467007.stm.
10. http://www/guardian.co.uk/business/2010/jan/23/kraft-cadbury-fairtrade.
11. http://www.tradingvisions.org/content/kraft-cadbury-takeover.
12. http://www.telegraph.co.uk/finance/newsbysector/retailandconsuer/7036463/
    Warren-Buffet-Krafts-11.9bn-takeover-of-Cadbury-is-a-bad-deal.html.

CHAPTER 7

Is It Too Late to Back Out?

What is wrong with changing your mind because the facts changed? But you have to be able to say why you changed your mind and how the facts changed.

—Lee Iacocca

So here we are—the chapter this book is all about, the *material adverse change* (MAC). As discussed in the Introduction, MAC clause is a legal provision normally found in mergers and acquisitions contracts. It allows a buyer to cancel an acquisition if the target company suffers a significant negative change in their financial position prior to closing the deal.

The clause is intended to protect the acquirer from major events that may make the target less attractive to buy. Large transactions often require a long period of time between actual agreement to buy (*signing*) and the completion of the transaction (*closing*). This time is used to obtain governmental or regulatory approvals, get shareholder consent to the transaction, arrange financing for the deal, or anything else that needs to be done prior to the new owners taking over running of the business.

During this period, the target company continues to function as it always has pending the completion of the merger, and is subject to the normal risks of its business, the economy, or acts beyond its control. The company continues to be run by the existing management team under their policies and procedures. This is a very risky period for a buyer. They have committed to buy the company at a firm price, but they can't manage the operations yet because formal title has not passed. The MAC is intended to protect the buyer should any "unusual" things happen during this period.

Each merger agreement that contains a MAC clause has a different definition of what, in its particular context, constitutes a material adverse change. This can be one of the most difficult parts of any contract negotiation. It is hard to anticipate the wide variety of things that could happen between signing and closing an agreement. A lot of time can be spent negotiating who takes the risk for these things—buyer or seller. Further, most deals are now taking longer to close given complexity of financial markets and increased time for regulatory approval of larger deals. So the period being protected has become longer, putting even more pressure on a properly defined MAC.

Historically, the MAC clause has been very broad, protecting buyers from a wide variety of negative events that could occur after signing. However, over the years the clause has been tightened up substantially with the list of events that qualify for a MAC decreasing each year. It really gets down to who has the negotiating leverage. With a target very much in demand by multiple buyers, the seller has leverage to reduce the MAC to very unusual items that are narrowly defined. However, in a situation with only one available buyer, and an anxious seller, the MAC may be much broader, protecting the buyer from a wide variety of outcomes.

Normally, invoking an MAC is a very legitimate way for the acquiring party to refuse to complete a contemplated acquisition. But more recently, sellers have started to sue buyers, claiming the events that actually occurred are not material enough to invoke the MAC clause. In the United States, much of this litigation occurs in the Delaware courts as many large American companies are organized under Delaware law. According to the precedents of that court, an acquirer seeking to avoid completion of a transaction based upon a MAC provision has to *positively* prove that a material adverse change as defined by the parties' agreement has in fact occurred.

CASE STUDY ONE: BANK OF AMERICA PURCHASES MERRILL LYNCH

But what does a business MAC look like, whom does it protect, and why doesn't it save more people from doing bad deals? Appendix A shows a very general MAC clause from when a nonprofit organization called Trinity International Foundation purchased a financial services, human resources, and administrative consultant to the nonprofit industry, called the American Public Medical Group. The legal language in Appendix A implies that the buyer should be protected after they buy the company but before they actually take over the business. These protections include:

- Mistakes made by the seller before the property was sold to the buyer:
  What if the seller entered into a major loss-making contract the day before they sold the company? With no protection, the buyer would have to pay the same price for the property with no ability to protect themselves from a loss-making contract.

  The buyer had most likely completed due diligence before putting in a firm offer to buy. However, they have very limited ability to control the activities of the seller between signing and closing to prevent material changes to what these reviewed. The MAC clause places liability on the seller for any unusual things they do between signing and closing.

  But the fundamental problem is how you define *unusual*. The seller may argue that entering into such contracts is very normal for their type of business and is "consistent with past practice." The buyer would argue that such a large contract signed immediately before closing is unusual. If proven right, the buyer could ask the seller to reverse the contract or to pay for the damages caused by this improper contract.

This is where company legal counsel can burn a lot of time and billable hours. In fairness to the lawyers, trying to define such nebulous terms as *unusual* and *standard practice* in writing and in terms that both parties agree to can be very hard. There are points of diminishing returns in any negotiation. I can't tell you how many late nights I spent at the negotiating table trying to manage all parties to a reasonable definition of words like *reasonable* without staying up all night!

■ Changes beyond anyone's control:

What if you purchased a company with its main manufacturing site on the Mississippi River and the river flooded the day before you were scheduled to close? The manufacturing site would be closed for several months during cleanup and sales would be irreparably harmed as a result. Whose liability is this? Well, in most MACs, liability would remain with the seller as it happened while they still owned the company. Normally there is a provision that if a natural disaster occurs between signing and closing, it is the seller's responsibility. But again, there is no standard answer to this question; it really comes down to the end results of the negotiation.

The MAC for the Trinity Foundation deal is *limited* by the following:

■ *Industry-specific events.* Given that the company being purchased is in the radio broadcasting industry, the buyer must accept responsibility for other risks common to radio companies.
■ *The economy.* Changes in the general economic condition are to be borne by the buyer. However, this example of the clause is very generic and might be harder to enforce if any issues surfaced.
■ *Regulatory.* In this deal, risk of changes in laws and regulations between signing and closing are borne by the buyer. In some highly regulated industries this exception would place a large exposure on the buyer if regulations did in fact change adversely between signing and closing.

Notice how simple the MAC clause is in the Trinity deal. Material events that are *not* covered are limited to industry-specific (media industry) issues, declines in general market conditions, new laws, or bad actions by the buyers. Even with these limitations, this MAC clause is very simple and straightforward. On the positive side, it is simple and easy to understand. On the negative side, it could lead to confusion over what actually constitutes a material enough change in the economy to allow the buyer to back out of the contract.

Compare this to the MAC clause from BofA Merrill signed on September 15, 2007, right before the financial crisis (see Appendix B). This MAC included significantly more detail and outlines multiple specific exclusions (i.e., places where the *buyer* has responsibility if unforeseen changes occur), including:

- Acts of terrorism or war:
  An act of terrorism or war could have a severe impact on the economy, your industry, and the company you want to buy. Should the buyer or seller bear the damages of a terrorist attack and/or a slowdown in the economy between signing and closing? Historically, such losses were taken by sellers, but they are being pushed to buyers in the more recent transactions as, tragically, acts of terrorism have become more common. While this clause is included in both the Trinity and BofA deals, it is much more detailed in BofA.
- Changes in accounting policies:
  Changes in the rules surrounding how results are recorded can have a significant impact on company value. In the BofA Merrill deal, this is something BofA agreed to take the full risk for.
- Changes in laws or regulations:
  The financial services sector has become highly regulated following the economic crisis. Dodd Frank and other rules were implemented to help protect against the large bank failures that occurred during the crisis. Many of these rules, while necessary to help prevent another recession, had a material negative impact on the results of financial institutions. By agreeing to be held responsible for any changes to laws or regulations that might impact Merrill, BofA was assuming potential risk given how quickly these regulations were changing at that time.
- Actions of the seller:
  This exception is very logical in that the seller will not be held responsible for damages from simply fulfilling their side of the contract or taking actions specifically requested by the buyer.

With all of these limitations, you may be wondering how BofA would have ever been able to invoke the MAC on the Merrill purchase, even if they wanted to. However, consider what happened to the global economy during the period between signing and closing for Bank of America/Merrill:

- Lehman Brothers bankruptcy filing
- Start of the Great Recession
- Bank liquidity drying up
- Over $1 trillion of stock market value lost for the year

More specifically, with respect to Merrill Lynch:

- Merrill reported losses of $5.1 billion for the third-quarter 2008 with another $5.3 billion expected for the fourth quarter. To make matters worse, management decided not to disclose this fourth-quarter anticipated loss to shareholders before they asked them to vote for final approval of the acquisition in mid-December.

- The merger agreement included a clause that Merrill executives were entitled to a total of $5.8 billion in bonuses regardless of how the company performed for 2008! BofA executives would later claim that they were "unaware" of this clause even though it was disclosed in the agreement.

Why didn't Ken Lewis invoke the MAC and back away from the purchase of Merrill? It was clear by early December that Merrill was not the same company that BofA had agreed to buy on September 15. Even with the detailed list of exclusions in the MAC language, BofA surely could have developed reasonable arguments as to why not to complete the deal. An analysis of the actual events during this time provides some insights why the deal still went through despite the reservations of all involved.

The board of Bank of America met in December to determine if they were going to invoke the MAC. Shareholders had already approved the deal two weeks earlier; however, they were unaware of the large loss pending at Merrill for the fourth quarter. The BofA board did know about this loss and the severe impact this could have on the combined entity, and they had to factor it into their decision whether to move forward.

But the board also faced a conflict. The government was pushing Ken Lewis hard to consummate the transaction for the good of the country and the global economy. A termination of the deal and subsequent failure of Merrill would be another surprise to an already tumultuous market and potentially bring the global economy down even further. The U.S. government argued that, by default, this would have a severe impact on BofA's operations. Therefore, to save the country, the global economy, and his own bank, Ken Lewis had to close the transaction. What an untenable position for any CEO to be put in.

Lewis was very appropriately concerned about his shareholders and asked the BofA attorneys to analyze the MAC clause relative to these unprecedented events. The attorneys opined that there were more than enough material changes in Merrill Lynch operations after the deal was signed to allow BofA to walk away from the deal under the MAC clause. At this point, the government became even more aggressive. Hank Paulson, then U.S. Treasury Secretary, said, "I'm going to be very blunt, we're supportive of BofA and we want to help, but...the government does not feel it's in your best interest for you to call a MAC, and we feel so strongly...we will remove the board and management if you call it."[1]

Lewis decided to deescalate the situation. He ultimately agreed to move forward with the deal, saying, "We are so intertwined with the United States that it is hard to separate what is good for the United States from what is good for Bank of America. Things could get a lot worse for America and for us and they are almost one and the same."[2]

At the same time, the U.S. government offered to support the deal further by guaranteeing some of the troubled assets. Paulson agreed to provide Merrill with over $100 billion to cover the anticipated losses that BofA could now incur on Merrill's most toxic assets. This helped further convince BofA to proceed with the deal. However, when BofA was asked for a written letter of support from the government, they were told that anything in writing would force public disclosure of the government guarantee. A public disclosure of this support could have caused the exact panic in the market that Paulson was trying to avoid by pushing for the Merrill deal to close.

In the end, Lewis and the board conceded. They did not have much of a choice. As Andrew Ross Sorkin paraphrased the government's position, "If you don't follow along, if you don't go with the program, you will not be part of this program any more. You will have to buy Merrill and we will make sure that happens up to and including removal of management and removal of the board."[3] Lewis was ultimately convinced that pursuing the deal was in the best interests of BofA. Lewis stated, "We decided that it was in the best interests of all involved to move forward."[4]

The failure to invoke the MAC and back away from this deal ultimately cost Lewis his job. In early 2009, the 2008 fourth-quarter losses for Merrill became public knowledge. The large bonuses owed to Merrill executives, despite the horrible financial results, became apparent. The government's financial support to the deal became public. Shareholders were furious that they did not know about any of these events when they were asked to approve the merger. They were extremely upset that Lewis moved forward on a deal that they believed was not in the best interests of their company. The BofA/Merrill acquisition is a classic example of a deal where the MAC could have been invoked and the deal terminated. But this was not done for some very understandable reasons.

CASE STUDY TWO: AT&T/T MOBILE

A second example of a post-signing event putting a deal in jeopardy is AT&T's March 2011 proposed $39 billion purchase of T-Mobile from Deutsche Telekom. AT&T agreed to pay $25 billion in cash and $14 billion in AT&T common stock to finance the transaction. AT&T had the right to increase the cash portion of its offer by up to $4 billion with a corresponding reduction in the stock component of the purchase. Deutsche Telekom would be allowed to appoint one representative to the AT&T board.

At a high level, the deal did make a lot of strategic sense. It would combine the global number-two and number-four wireless carriers, adding scale in a very competitive market. The combined entity would surpass Verizon as the largest wireless carrier in the United States. AT&T argued that the positives of the deal included:

- It addressed the impending shortage of wireless spectrum for mobile broadband networks, devices, applications, and content for both companies.
- It allowed AT&T to extend its latest 4G spectrum to more than 97 percent of the U.S. population.
- It provided 4G spectrum access to T-Mobile's 34 million subscribers. (AT&T had 96 million subscribers at that time.)
- It improved network capacity and quality of service for customers of both companies.
- German-owned T-Mobile, the only major foreign-controlled U.S. telecom network, was to become part of a U.S.-based company, securing these valuable spectrum assets within the United States.
- The venture was anticipated to create 5,000 call center jobs in the United States should the deal close.

A combination of AT&T and T-Mobile would make it very difficult for the third largest carrier, Sprint, to compete. Sprint had already been losing money for months after aggressively offering better pricing than the competition to try to improve market share. Another impetus for the deal was the bleak prospects for T-Mobile without a merger or acquisition. T-Mobile on a stand-alone basis was in a very difficult financial position, as it was struggling to compete with the larger carriers, and Deutsche Telekom indicated that it would not invest any more in the company.

The big unknown in any deal like this in a critical industry, with very large players consolidating, is whether U.S. antitrust regulators will let the deal go through. Other carriers and public-interest groups will normally argue that the concentration of power from a merger into fewer players, in this case two of the top-five largest cell phone carriers in the United States, will reduce the competitive landscape and ultimately drive up pricing for consumers.

Strangely enough, even with this regulatory and consumer pressure, AT&T management agreed to pay a $3.0 billion cash breakup fee if the transaction did not close for regulatory reasons. In addition, they agreed to transfer to T-Mobile certain wireless spectrum and provide a roaming agreement to T-Mobile on terms favorable to both parties even if the deal never happened. The total value of the breakup fee was estimated to be *$4 to $6 billion.* Given the vagaries of the courts and the nebulous definitions of *anticompetitive*, this was a massive risk for AT&T to take.

The AT&T/T-Mobile stock purchase agreement stated:

> *The Stock Purchase Agreement contains certain termination rights for each of the T-Mobile, AT&T and Deutsche Telekom and, in the event that the stock purchase agreement is terminated because of failure to obtain regulatory approval, AT&T may become obligated to pay Deutsche Telekom $3 billion in cash, enter into a roaming agreement with Deutsche Telekom on terms favorable to both parties and transfer to Deutsche Telekom certain wireless AWS spectrum that the Company does not need for its initial LTE roll-out.*[5]

In layman's terms, AT&T had promised $3 billion in cash and another $3 billion in spectrum value if the deal did not go through for regulatory or other reasons. AT&T was making a massive bet for a deal subject to such intense regulatory scrutiny.

As expected, the regulatory discussions were long and detailed. Many of the states directly impacted by the merger expressed early support for the deal, including Alabama, Arkansas, Georgia, Kentucky, Michigan, Mississippi, North Dakota, South Dakota, Utah, West Virginia, and Wyoming. They saw a benefit to their state economies and local constituents from increased wireless buildout, providing greater coverage to more consumers and the creation of jobs for the local communities. As a result, a small contingent of 15 U.S. House of Representatives Democrats encouraged President Obama to support the deal.

Despite this pressure, the Department of Justice strongly objected to the merger on the basis that the combination of AT&T and T-Mobile would result in tens of millions of consumers all across the United States facing higher prices, fewer choices, and lower quality products for mobile wireless services. Deputy Attorney General James M. Cole, Department of Justice, stated,

> *Consumers across the country, including those in rural areas and those with lower incomes, benefit from competition among the nation's wireless carriers, particularly the four remaining national carriers. This lawsuit seeks to ensure that everyone can continue to receive the benefits of that competition.*[6]

The Department of Justice also argued that regional wireless providers would not be able to effectively compete against a combined AT&T and T-Mobile. It stated that the $39 billion AT&T proposed to invest in buying

T-Mobile would be better spent enhancing its own network. "T-Mobile has been an important source of competition, including through innovation and quality enhancements such as the roll-out of the first nationwide high-speed data network," stated Sharis Pozen, acting chief of Justice's antitrust division.

Attorney General Eric T. Schneiderman of New York stated the acquisition would reduce access to low-cost options and the newest broadband-based technologies for businesses and consumers and joined Department of Justice in blocking the deal. He claimed that the merger would violate federal antitrust laws and damage competition in both New York and national wireless markets.

Federal Communications Commission (FCC) Chairman Julius Genachowski stated:

> *Competition is an essential component of the FCC's statutory public interest analysis, and although our process is not complete, the record before this agency also raises serious concerns about the impact of the proposed transaction on competition. Vibrant competition in wireless services is vital to innovation, investment, economic growth and job creation, and to drive our global leadership in mobile. Competition fosters consumer benefits, including more choices, better service and lower prices.*[7]

The commission argued that if they allowed the merger to happen, AT&T would control more than 50 percent of the 17 metropolitan markets.

In July 2011, AT&T informed the FCC that they would submit new economic models to measure the effectiveness and benefits of a merger with T-Mobile. As a result, the FCC stopped the 180-day approval process until AT&T formally presented these new models. Bob Quinn, AT&T's SVP of Regulation, stated,

> *The engineering and economic models we have provided the Commission confirm the extensive capacity gains and corresponding consumer benefits that the combination of AT&T's and T-Mobile's complementary assets will produce. Once approved, this merger will unleash billions of dollars in badly needed investment and will create many thousands of well-paying jobs.*[8]

To further bolster their case, AT&T management agreed to sell off 25 percent of T-Mobile's business after closing and promised to not raise existing T-Mobile prices. This is often a tactic taken by buyers in large national or global deals. By selling off a large piece of the acquired company, the new entity's market share and ability to control prices is mitigated. Whether it is at the suggestion of the regulators or management, the sale of major divisions will often get the deal over the finish line from an antitrust perspective.

AT&T had hoped these efforts would allow the merger to get done. But even with this, the U.S. Department of Justice continued to argue that the combination would create a duopoly in the wireless market with AT&T and Verizon controlling 90 percent of the wireless market's profit. Competitors continued to complain and lobby Washington against the deal happening. Sprint sued AT&T on the basis that the deal would have given AT&T a significant lead in the number of subscribers, way ahead of even its closest competitor, Verizon.

In September 2011 the federal government filed suit as well. The Justice Department's antitrust lawsuit emphasizes three big points: (1) Consumers will inevitably pay more when they have fewer wireless carriers to choose from, (2) business and government contracts will have fewer bidders, resulting in less competition and higher prices, and (3) the market was so well-established nationally that nobody else would be able to fill the number-four spot behind AT&T, Verizon, and Sprint.

I present this detailed sequence of events to show how complicated and lengthy the debates around nebulous issues such as noncompetition can be. And think about to the distractions to the individual companies while these high-level debates were underway. Management transition teams had been set up to determine the mechanics of how to merge the companies. Decisions were being made about who would fill key roles after the deal closed. Debates on things ranging from office locations to human resource policies to the strategy of the combined entity were underway, all at a time when the certainty of the deal actually happening was becoming more unclear by the day.

Given all of this regulatory uncertainty over a number of months, why would any buyer expose themselves and their company to this uncertainty, never mind a $6 billion potential penalty for circumstances largely out of their control? Why did AT&T agree to this clause, or at a minimum not get a MAC clause that allowed them to withdraw from the deal immediately if regulatory approval could not be obtained? According to Thomson Reuters Data, at 15.4 percent of the total value of the deal, this breakup fee was the largest ever agreed to for two parties attempting to merge. The fact that they did it in such a regulatory-sensitive industry like Telecom makes the agreement even more unusual.

At the start of the deal AT&T must have had a high level of confidence that they could get regulatory approval. But in transactions like this, man-agement always need to be careful about areas that are not fully under their control. Things like paying more for a property, cutting cost, relocating facilities, and so forth are all arguably under the control of the buyer. But areas where independent bodies like U.S. regulators have the final say, regardless of your arguments, can create a binary outcome that is not in your favor.

In this case, the regulatory debate culminated in late November 2011 when AT&T and T-Mobile announced they were withdrawing their application to the FCC to merge their cell phone operations. The parties realized that, despite their initial high expectations, the regulators would never approve this deal. While the two parties stated that they would continue to pursue other means to get the deal approved, it now appeared very unlikely they would ever receive the antitrust approval needed to close.

As a result, AT&T announced a $4 billion charge against earnings for payment of the breakup fee to Deutsche Telekom. Craig Moffett, an analyst at Sanford Bernstein, stated that the withdrawal of the FCC application "is a tacit acknowledgement by AT&T that this story is all but over. The fat lady hasn't started singing yet, but she's holding the mike and the band is about to play."[9]

CASE STUDY THREE: VERIZON BIDS FOR YAHOO

A final, more recent, example of unexpected events between signing and closing can be seen in Verizon's bid to purchase 100 percent of Yahoo's core editorial and advertising businesses. First announced in July 2016, the now-number-one wireless carrier in the United States, Verizon, bid $4.8 billion for Yahoo's ad and content business. Verizon planned to build scale from digital advertising on mobile devices as growth in their traditional telecom business continued to decline. With over one billion users visiting Yahoo for sports scores, financial news, email, or other services, this would provide a great platform for Verizon to expand their digital presence.

Yahoo management also believed that Verizon was a nice follow-on acquisition to the AOL business they acquired a year earlier for $4.4 billion. Although AOL failed to make a lot of progress as a more traditional digital content company, it did manage to combine programmed ad buying with the targeting tools needed for video. The core editorial and advertising businesses within Yahoo were a nice complement to this business. Analyst Craig Moffett stated, "Verizon is trying to pivot its business from analog to digital. Verizon believes that a combined AOL/Yahoo would provide the digital advertising platform they need to execute their video reinvention strategy."[10]

But subsequent to the deal being agreed to, Yahoo disclosed that they had suffered a breach of company data in over 500 million user accounts.

The incidents happened in 2013 and 2014, but unfortunately were not discovered until after Verizon and Yahoo had signed the purchase agreement. Verizon argued that this was clearly a material adverse change that was not disclosed at the time of the deal. Since they did not know about this liability when they signed the agreement, Verizon asked for a $925 million reduction in the purchase price to cover the potential exposure.

There could clearly be material liability to the combined entity from this issue. In fact, Yahoo still faces dozens of lawsuits related to the theft of user data. In 2013, hackers stole information that included weakly encrypted passwords and one billion consumer accounts and then sold the information online. The following year, another set of hackers believed to be sponsored by a foreign government stole similar information on 500 million accounts.

After considerable debate, the two parties agreed to share the ultimate liability for these data breaches. Verizon's claim for the breach was reduced from $925 million to $350 million. While Yahoo had tremendous leverage under the MAC language, they still wanted the deal to happen so they had to arrive at a pragmatic solution. Marni Walden, Verizon EVP for Product Innovation, stated,

> We have always believed this acquisition makes strategic sense. We look forward to moving ahead expeditiously so that we can welcome Yahoo's tremendous talent and assets into our expanding portfolio in the digital advertising space.[11]

This is a good example where, even with great contractual protections around a MAC or other issues, a buyer may have to make concessions to get a deal done. Had Verizon held out for a full $925 million, the deal may have never closed. Despite the data breaches, Verizon remained intrigued with the massive digital audiences brought in by Yahoo. They were able to leverage the data breaches to lower the purchase price, but clearly believed that the incidents were not material enough to sideline the entire deal. Verizon needed the deal too badly for other competitive reasons.

CONCLUSION

So what does all of this mean? The material adverse change has gone from a clause rarely even considered to a major focus of most large transactions completed after the Great Recession. The protections provided to buyers have narrowed as the world has become more turbulent, both politically and in business. Not only are the MAC clauses becoming more restrictive, but it is also getting harder to enforce what is in the contract due to regulatory and political pressures.

This puts increased importance on buyers to do their due diligence and to really understand what they are actually buying *before* they sign the contract. If you can no longer back out after signing the deal, this period between signing and closing becomes even more critical. It puts CEOs like Ken Lewis under significant exposure from post-signing events they simply can't control, yet they are legally or morally bound to go ahead and complete the transaction.

Tighter MACs will also increase the role and influence of government in these situations. As we saw in AT&T/T-Mobile, the U.S. government has increasing influence on whether a deal goes through and, as a result, whether AT&T will have to pay a multibillion-dollar breakup fee to T-Mobile. As we saw in BofA/Merrill, Ken Lewis appeared to have the legal right to invoke the MAC and cancel the deal. However, the more-than-subtle pressure from the government convinced Lewis and his board to move forward with an acquisition where they had serious doubts.

Finally, these cases show that it is not always what is written in the contract that drives the answer. As we saw in Verizon/Yahoo, there can be softer and legitimate reasons why a buyer wants to move forward with a deal even after material adverse events surface after the contract is signed. This then becomes not a detailed legal analysis of the contract language, but a pragmatic discussion between two business leaders on how to make the most out of a bad situation and still arrive at a pragmatic result.

No one is quite sure how the MAC clause will evolve from here. A more unstable world will likely increase the need for clear, detailed MAC clauses to determine how and when a buyer can back away from a deal. However, it is this same turbulent environment that drives sellers to be more restrictive on letting buyers off the hook for changes in the business environment that they can't control. Government continues to show an increased willingness to get involved and to interpret these MAC clauses. All of this will increase the uncertainty of these deals, make transactions more complex, and limit the ability of buyers to back away from contracts that no longer make sense.

NOTES

1. Testimony of Ken Lewis to Andrew Cuomo, Attorney General of New York, February 26, 2009.
2. *Breaking the Bank*, June 16, 2009, written and directed by Michael Kirk.
3. Ibid.
4. Ibid.

5. ATT SEC filing, March 2011
6. "Justice Department Moves to Block AT&T, T-Mobile Merger," The Carmody Business, August 31, 2011.
7. "Justice Department Moves to Block AT&T, T-Mobile Merger," The Carmody Business, August 31, 2011.
8. "FCC Restarts the Shot Clock on AT&T, T-Mobile Merger," Paul Barbagallo, Bloomberg, August 31, 2011.
9. "AT&T Merger with T-Mobile Faces Setbacks," Edward Wyatt and Jenna Wortham, November 24, 2011
10. "Verizon Sought $925 Million Discount for Yahoo Merger, got $350 Million," *Technology News*, March 13, 2017.
11. "Verizon's Cost to Buy Yahoo Is Reduced to $350 Million," *New York Times*, February 22, 2017.

CHAPTER 8

How to Negotiate a Better Deal

My father said: 'You must never try to make all the money that's in a deal. Let the other fellow make some money, too, because if you have a reputation for always making all the money, you won't have many deals.'

—J. Paul Getty

remember one morning before work several years ago, when my family was living in London. My youngest daughter, Megan, nine years old at the time, was struggling to get out of bed in time for school. She very much wanted to sleep late, stay home, and have a fun day. When I tried to wake her, she resisted. Her first response was the ever-popular child excuse of "Daddy, I am sick." After I felt her cool forehead, she admitted she felt fine. She then argued that the long "tube" ride to school was too much for such a small girl to handle. Megan then promised to do all of her homework and read all day as opposed to watching television if I let her stay home. Finally, she *promised* to go to school the following day. However, I did not relent, and she grudgingly crawled out of her nice warm bed to get ready for the day.

When I went downstairs for breakfast, my 13-year-old daughter, Rachel, did not want to eat the oatmeal I had made for her. At first, Rachel said she was not hungry. Her second argument was that she did not like oatmeal. Her third argument was that I was simply a very poor cook. However, Rachel did agree to eat some fruit in lieu of the oatmeal, which seemed like a reasonable compromise to me.

As my oldest daughter, Lauren, was leaving the house, she asked for £80 to buy an Abercrombie & Fitch sweater on the way home from school. Of course she *needed* the sweater right away and it had to be an Abercrombie sweater to keep her warm! After some back-and-forth, I eventually agreed to give her £40. She could either buy a cheaper sweater or use four weeks of her own allowance money if she really had to have the A&F sweater. Another problem solved as Lauren cheerfully left for school.

On my way out the door, my wife, Amy, asked what time I would be home that evening. I explained that I had an important dinner that would keep me out until at least 9:00. Amy pointed out that she, too, had plans at 7:00 and that this would cause a problem for her. Again after some back-and-forth, I agreed to come home immediately after pre-dinner drinks were over, arriving by 6:30 so she could enjoy her evening as well.

My objective here is not to bore you with tales about my family—I am sure you have many of your own to tell. However, the four stories do illustrate that most things in life are a negotiation. On this particular day, I had four separate negotiations *before I even left the house for work!* I often ask my MBA students to raise their hand in class if they feel like they entered into a negotiation that day. Very few hands go up. But after explaining what a negotiation actually entails, the entire class admits they have likely had more than one on just that day. From simply posturing with a stranger as to who holds the door for the other, to negotiating the terms of an apartment lease, everything is a negotiation.

One of the most critical things to being a good negotiator is to simply be aware that you are in a negotiation and then to act accordingly. How can you be an effective negotiator if you are not even conscious that you are in a negotiation? This can lead to disappointing results in business as well as your personal life. The concepts we discuss in this chapter should help you in any M&A scenario, but also in the hundreds of small and large negotiations most people have each year.

Here is a second example from a business context. In the middle part of my career, I worked in the business development group for a large corporation. I had spent months analyzing the acquisition of a large global financial services firm that was a perfect fit with our business. The due diligence included many late hours in the office and weekends away from my family. Although there were many factors that would weigh in on performance review for the year, closing this particular $1 billion-plus transaction would certainly help to improve my review, my standing in the company, and my overall compensation for the year.

The sales process for this property had started with over 50 bidders. After a first round of due diligence, the field was reduced to six bidders. These parties were allowed to meet with company management and review a limited set of books and records before submitting a non-binding bid for the property. After this process, the bidders were reduced from six parties down to two. My company was one of the final two, and the seller's investment bank indicated we were the preferred bidder. We had done everything right. We had spent ample time with management of the target company to build trust. We had been reasonable in our negotiations around legal points in the agreement. We had offered a fair price for the company. We had received quick internal approval for the transaction and provided a timely response to the seller. And we had arranged for the capital to close the transaction quickly and efficiently, leaving little uncertainty with the seller that we would actually go through with the deal.

All we could do now was wait. The tension was incredible. The team and I had put a ton of time and effort into this transaction, which would now have a binary outcome. The seller's banker indicated that we were "well positioned" and would hear something next week on who the winner was. On Monday morning, I received the call. I knew this was a good sign. In situations like these, no news is usually bad news, so I was happy that he called. I was prepared to take the good news.

However, the banker was still surprisingly neutral. He explained that we were indeed the preferred bidder. The target company really wanted to partner and work with us to grow together. But he indicated that, unfortunately, we were not the highest bidder. Another buyer had agreed to pay a slightly higher premium for the property than my company. But since we were the preferred bidder, he wanted to provide "one last chance" for us to win.

At this point I took a deep breath and asked how much our bid would need to go up to win. The amount was $10mm or about 2 percent of the purchase price. I viewed this as very good news. After all, $10mm was relatively small in the context of a $500 million investment. Surely we would pay $10 million extra after all the work we had done. This company was a perfect fit for us, and we could not let this deal get away. As I hung up the phone, I was very happy that we had essentially won the deal. I was sure that I would be calling the banker back before lunch, agreeing to pay the $10mm and starting to celebrate.

That was until I went to see my boss and explain the situation. He reminded me that $10mm is still a heck of a lot of money. He warned me not to get caught "anchoring and adjusting." This is a negotiation concept where one of the parties can lose perspective around incremental increases to an overall much higher purchase price. In the context of a $500mm deal, $10mm might not seem material. However, if someone were to give you $10mm tomorrow, it would certainly seem like a lot of money! In a negotiation, keeping perspective around the absolute dollars being spent as opposed to the relative amount of increases is very important.

My boss presumed that the other side was using the first technique of negotiating—the bluff. He did not believe that another bidder was truly offering a higher price than we were. In fact, he believed that we would win the deal whether or not we paid another $10mm. The seller was merely trying to squeeze another $10mm out of us as they knew we were very anxious to buy the property. I made the counterargument to my boss. After all the time and money we spent on the deal, were we really willing to take the chance of losing for a mere $10mm? Why take a chance of losing a very appealing acquisition at this point?

This is where you enter one of the toughest parts of any negotiation—patience, nerve, and persistence. It showed the contrast of an experienced negotiator like my boss relative to a newcomer like me. My boss had been through these situations before. He was able to keep his perspective and leverage experience from past deals. Interestingly, he said that he would leave the decision up to me as I had spent the most time on the deal and had put my heart and soul into its success. If I wanted to feel better immediately, I should call the banker, agree to the deal, and go out for a nice lunch. But he emphasized that the phone call and my good feeling would cost our company $10mm. I knew the answer—I had to wait.

I waited all day Monday without making the call. I had some sleepless nights and waited all the way to Thursday of that week. Finally, the call came on Thursday afternoon. Once the banker called back rather than waiting for my response, I knew the leverage had shifted back to me. If he had such a strong second bidder, why was he calling me again? Why wouldn't he just go with that bidder when he did not hear back from me immediately? He sheepishly asked me where we had ended up on purchase price. The banker could now only make a halfhearted attempt to get another $10mm. He would not have called back if another buyer had truly bid more. He would have taken the other offer.

When I explained that I did not have approval to go any higher, the banker said he would call me back. In less than an hour I received a call that we were "lucky" and the seller had agreed to sell to us even though we were not the highest bidder. We will never know whether this was true or whether it was a bluff, although I have my suspicions. But it does not matter. The important point is that negotiation is all about being patient and holding your ground when it should be held. Fighting your own emotions and avoiding emotional responses to issues is critical to negotiation success.

TEN BEST PRACTICES FOR EFFECTIVE NEGOTIATION

Effective negotiation takes practice, consistency, and an ability to emotionally remove yourself from the discussion. Full books have been written on the art of negotiation. But my personal ten best practices for an effective negotiation in an M&A context are as follows:

1. Keep Your Eye on the Ball

It is very easy to lose perspective in any negotiation. M&A deals often involve late nights at the attorney's office negotiating hundreds of points. At times people get competitive and overly concerned with winning every point rather than focusing on the important issues.

For example, I thought I was doing quite well in one negotiation of a multimillion-dollar purchase of a company that manufactured storage tanks for underground waste. I was able to negotiate protection that the seller would continue to provide services until we were able to establish our own payroll system. I reached agreement that we could keep the seller's corporate headquarters for our staff. I was able to negotiate the ability to use that seller's company logo for six months. I had won most of the points. I believed that I had become the "master negotiator." The only point I gave up was that the seller would not be responsible for environmental liabilities after we closed the deal. But I had won the majority of the points up for discussion.

Unfortunately, the point I gave away was massively more important than all of the points I won put together. An environmental issue could cause unlimited amounts of damages for my company. What if the company's tanks had leaked and contaminated the underground water supply and we did not know about it? Such latent liabilities are often present at closing, but the buyer and seller are not aware of them because they have not surfaced yet. But they can certainly become major issues after closing. Without contract protection, I was exposing my company to unlimited exposure on issues that could be massive. I had essentially agreed that we would pay for environmental claims whether they were our fault or not!

I failed to recognize that it is not the *quantity* of arguments you win in a negotiation; it is the *quality* of those you win. Luckily, we did not encounter any environmental claims with this purchase, but it was a good lesson to me about focusing on important issues as the ones to win.

A second example was the purchase of a subsidiary of a large parent company. I was winning all of the issues. The seller agreed to cover all environmental issues fully. The seller guaranteed that the senior management team would come over to our organization. They even agreed to reimburse our legal costs if we had any legal disputes after closing. We were very fortunate to get such a comprehensive list of protections.

The night before we were scheduled to close, I took one last look at the contract. The party that stands behind guarantees like these in an M&A contract is called the *indemnitor*. For example, if we had exposure for environmental claims, the indemnitor would reimburse us. The entity labeled as the indemnitor was the sole party that had the obligation to pay us back. As I read the document I had a sick feeling in my stomach. In this case, the indemnitor was not the parent company that was worth millions of dollars. The other side had created a subsidiary with only $100,000 of cash as the indemnitor to provide a guarantee on issues that could total millions of dollars. The ultimate parent company had no legal obligation to pay whatsoever.

Why is this important? Suppose I ended up with a $5mm environmental claim that the seller had agreed to cover. Since my indemnitor was only worth $100,000, they would never be able to pay the claim. They would likely file for bankruptcy, and the parent company would write off the division. Although the parent company had sufficient money to pay, it had not guaranteed the contractual representations of its subsidiary itself; therefore, it had no liability.

Now I knew why I had been so successful in the negotiation—because I would never receive more than $100,000 regardless of the level of actual claims. The seller had effectively capped their total exposure for all of the indemnities they had given me at $100,000, so they didn't really care about the promises they made. The seller's team had outnegotiated me. They had appealed to my ego. I was happy that I was winning all of the points, but I would have put my company in jeopardy if I had signed the contact as is.

2. Remain Patient

When Amy and I were just starting out, we found the "perfect" house to buy. It was in the right neighbourhood, had the right number of bedrooms, a great backyard, and so on. There was only one problem—the price. It was listed about 10 percent over what we thought the value was and what we could reasonably afford. The seller was unwilling to negotiate on price at all, as the house had been on the market for only two weeks.

Amy and I had a long discussion. On the one hand, it was perfect for us, and we had been looking for months. We felt we would never find a home as nice as this one. I argued that we needed to move forward. It was only 10 percent more, and house prices were rising. Certainly we would be back into the money in several months.

But Amy was the voice of reason. We did not have to move quickly. Although the apartment we were in was small and cramped, we could certainly continue to live there for some time and be happy. There were new homes coming on the market every day to increase our options.

Luckily, I listened to Amy, and we did not buy the house. Only two weeks later a new house came on the market that was even better. It was in a nicer neighbourhood, had one more bedroom, and was in better condition. To top it all off, it was 20 percent lower than the first home we liked.

We purchased the home, loved it, and stayed in it for five years. We realized a substantial gain from our original purchase price when we sold. By listening to my wife and remaining patient, we had made the right business decision. In hindsight this all looks logical and easy. However, emotions, impatience, and ego would likely have driven me to buy the first house if not for the sound judgment of Amy. It is hard to be patient. It is hard to keep things in perspective. It is hard to pass on something you really want. But to be a good negotiator you have to learn how to do this. You can't look back; you must move forward. In almost all cases a better opportunity will eventually surface, even if you think that it never will.

This also happens in the world of M&A time after time. As we discussed in Chapter 1, did Fred Goodwin continue to pursue ABN AMRO because he thought it was a good deal, or because he did not want to lose it to Barclays? When would RBS ever have such a great opportunity again to buy a global, well-respected bank? When would Goodwin have another chance to make a name for himself by completing the largest acquisition in history? We will never know whether a lack of patience played into the process; however, it must have had something to do with Goodwin's decision to move forward. Had he waited, he could likely have bought much better properties at much better prices than what he committed to in the battle for ABN AMRO.

3. Listen

I fundamentally believe that having the ability and the willingness to listen is one of the most overlooked qualities in interpersonal relations. Many of us, and especially CEOs of major corporations, have large egos. What could someone else possibly say that would benefit us if we already have all of the answers? We spend our time in meetings trying to prove to everyone how smart we are versus getting input from those around the table and learning.

Albert Einstein said, "If A equals success, then the formula is $A = X + Y + Z$, with X being work, Y play, and Z keeping your mouth shut." This is especially true in a negotiating setting. One can learn a lot about a person's position on a particular issue by watching their body motions and the tone and context of what they say. Paying attention to others in the room can be more enlightening than anything you can possibly have to say.

I was once involved in the negotiation of the purchase of a global cable television company. The lead attorney on the other side of the table, Martin, was a seasoned veteran of multiple deals. He showed very little emotion, which made him very hard to read. Many days we would work late into the evening to continue negotiating. At around 8:00 P.M. each night and every 15 minutes thereafter, Martin's junior colleague would come into the negotiating room. Martin would stop the discussion in midstream, quickly consult with his colleague, and then move on.

After a while, this became very distracting. My imagination started to run away from me. Was Martin receiving important, real-time information on our deal? Was he checking on the status of another important deal? Was he merely trying to disrupt the flow of the discussions and to put me off guard? I tried my best to not let this bother me. But I found myself losing track of the conversation and missing points. Although I did not give away any major points because of this, it certainly did not help my focus.

Deal teams often go out to celebrate together once the deal is signed and complete. Both sides have worked hard and hopefully arrived at a fair outcome. On this deal, we went out to a nice restaurant the week after the deal closed. I had to know what was so important to Martin that he needed updates every 15 minutes. He was a tough, seasoned negotiator and I thought I could learn a lot from him. So as dessert was being served, I got up my nerve to ask him.

It turns out that Martin was a rabid New York Yankees fan. His colleague was actually updating him on the score of the Yankees games every 15 minutes! Martin admitted that the messages were to serve two purposes. One was that he desperately wanted to know the score. The second was indeed to disrupt the flow of the discussion and to distract me from the issues at hand.

Listening closely, avoiding distractions, and a proper interpretation of what is being said can be invaluable in determining the positions of the other side.

4. Honesty Is the Best Policy

I have found that people have long memories in business and in life. Being honest and up-front in negotiations is critical not only to one's reputation, but to the reputation of the organization you represent. You might get a short-term benefit by working on the fringes of true honesty. It might get you the upper hand in the current deal. However, the long-term consequences can be disastrous. It only takes one instance to ruin your reputation. People will remember it on the next deal as well.

You often see this in an M&A negotiation. At the start of the deal, the power resides with the seller. In today's competitive market, there are usually multiple bidders for each property up for sale. However, the auction process gradually narrows down the parties involved until you get down to one with whom you will negotiate a contract. In many cases, sellers have time pressure on completing a transaction as well. They may need to get it done by the end of the year for accounting purposes, or they may need to get it done quickly because they need the cash.

As the process continues to eliminate bidders, the power shifts from seller to buyer. The seller has fewer alternatives as the pool of bidders is reduced. Fewer bidders continue to complete due diligence. A lot of time is spent negotiating contracts, obtaining regulatory approvals, and arranging funds for payment. By the end of contract negotiation, there is usually only one party who can close within the time deadline. Starting over would be costly and frustrating, so the motivation to close with this lone buyer is now extraordinarily high.

Some buyers have been known to use this leverage to their advantage at the last minute. These deals invariably come right up to the deadline. In more than one instance, I have been scrambling to get final points agreed to in the contract by 5:00 P.M. on Friday night before the banks close and we can no longer process the wire transfer. Buyers suspect that the seller is more likely to agree to anything at the last minute than they have been during the entire process.

Let's take an example. Suppose it is Friday afternoon at 12:00 P.M. and the deal needs to close that day. A party uses this leverage at the last minute to request that the buyer's protection for environmental claims go from $10 million to $20 million, even though they had formally agreed to $10 million two days earlier as part of a concession on multiple points. What is a seller to do? If they *have* to sign the deal when the banks close at 5:00 P.M., they have nowhere else to go. The seller may feel tremendous pressure to start conceding points if they really need the money and no other bidders are around. They must deal with you.

But while this behavior may work in the short term, in the long term it can be extremely damaging to you and your firm and the ability to win deals going forward. The M&A market is small, and people have long memories. The next time you bid on a property, you will be the *last* person the seller wants to deal with. They will not believe the terms of your offer as you changed them at the last minute on your last deal. In the M&A profession, personal credibility and trust is critical to being effective in the long term. What you gain today by being dishonest, you lose multiples of in the longer term.

5. Be Sensitive to the Other Side

Let's go back to my earlier example. I had to tell the banker that we could not raise our price by another $10 million, but we still wanted the deal. But I found a way to connect with him and still get my point across. I explained that I fully understood why the price should have been $10mm higher and that this was a reasonable request on his part. However, I could not convince my board of directors or my boss to raise the bid despite his reasonable concerns.

While this may seem a bit weak, it does serve a purpose. It helps your negotiating partner save face. You are saying no, but also agreeing with his position. I could have gotten emotional and said, "There is no way in the world we are raising price and you are crazy to even ask!" This would have delivered the same outcome, but with high collateral damage to banker's ego and our ability to do business on future deals going forward. No one wants to be embarrassed in a negotiation, especially when the other side has effectively called their bluff. By being collaborative, but still firm on price, the outcome for both sides was much more pleasant.

6. Check Your Ego at the Door

Emotions and ego can often get in the way of a good negotiation. It is very easy to lose perspective and enter into a battle with your adversary on the other side of the table. But the best, seasoned negotiators rarely show any emotion. Why let the other side know you are upset about a particular point? Why reveal that this point is so critical to you? Rather, the better approach is to stay calm and rational, but still prove your position. This also has the benefit of accentuating the impact of the few times you do lose your patience, instead of it becoming a normal course event.

You have to always remember that negotiations around M&A are not a personal contest. Rather, it is a process to find a fair compromise on the important things that the buyer and seller need to get out of the process. Some of the best negotiations that I have been involved with are when the other side thinks they have won a personal battle between competitors. I try my best to remove my ego and competitiveness, focus on the big picture, and not get emotional. This has worked particularly well for me in getting to a reasonable answer with the other side.

7. Find Ways for Mutual Gain

In many cases, things that are important to you may not be important to the other side, and vice-versa. These make for the most efficient negotiations as points can be traded off very easily. The toughest negotiations are when both sides put critical importance on the same issues. This makes it very hard to trade issues as neither side wants to give them up.

I was once involved in the purchase of a business that financed real estate. The seller did not own any of the real estate; it was only a lender to real estate owned by others. But we noticed something unusual when we started to go through due diligence on the firm's balance sheet. There was only one asset listed as owned by the firm. It was an apartment right next to the business's corporate headquarters. Owning real estate was not part of the corporate strategy of the division we were buying. Further, whenever this topic came up, the other side became agitated and pleaded that we purchase this apartment as part of the deal.

But I had learned how to negotiate. Rather than responding right away, I kept delaying this issue. As the deal process continued, the other side became more and more worried about getting rid of the corporate apartment. At this point, I knew I had an area that was of critical value to the seller but that was not important to me. The purchase of an apartment was nothing in the context of a hundred-million-dollar deal. However, I was smart enough to realize that I could leverage it for something that was important to me.

In this case, I was able to trade buying the apartment in exchange for the seller providing me with an unlimited warranty around environment protection. This had massive value for me and my company. I had traded a $250,000 purchase of an apartment for a guarantee against potentially millions of dollars of environmental exposure to my company. This is the essence of a good negotiation—trading on points that are relevant to each party. Proper negotiation is easier when there are a fair amount of points that are important to one side and not important to the other.

As an aside, you may be wondering why the apartment was so important to the seller. It turns out that the CEO of the division we were buying was using this apartment at the company's expense, but without any permission from the Corporate Office. He had been able to hide the fact that he was using the apartment rent free for years. Had the apartment not been sold with the business, it would have been apparent to all involved that this the CEO was doing something wrong. From his perspective, it was critical that the apartment be sold and from our side, it really did not matter that much. This is a good example of where both sides can be happy with trading an issue.

8. Know and Use Your Leverage

A few years ago, my wife, Amy, and I decided to move to a moderately larger house around the corner from ours. I was relatively indifferent as I liked the house we were in, but Amy absolutely loved this new house and "had to have it." Unfortunately, we both agreed that the sales price was about 10 percent over its true value and it had just been listed for sale, making the seller less likely to negotiate on price until they had tested the market.

We scheduled a tour of the house with the seller's real estate agent. As the agent walked us through the house, Amy kept making comments about how she absolutely loved the lawn, the bedrooms, the space in the living room, the backyard pool, and so on. As she continued to speak, the smile on the seller agent's face became wider and wider. When we went upstairs and saw the "his-and-hers" walk-in closets, Amy said, "Bob, if you don't buy this house for me, I will divorce you!" While I don't think she really meant it, this statement had a massive effect on the position of the seller's agent. The leverage around buying this house immediately transferred from us to the seller's agent. She realized that Amy was willing to buy the home at any price.

We had broken one of the cardinal rules of negotiating. If the other side does not truly believe you are willing to walk away from the deal, they will continue to negotiate hard on all points. Why would they give any points away if they know you have already decided to move forward? In this case, the seller now had all of the leverage.

But sometimes you can create your own leverage in negotiations. I purposely waited for several days until the agent called us back for feedback. I bluffed a little bit and said Amy had left the purchase decision up to me.

I told the agent that while we did like her house, there were several others on the market that were almost as good, but at significantly lower prices. What was I trying to do? I was attempting to convince the seller that we would not move forward on her listing at a crazy price, and that we had alternatives. After the events during the tour, I could not credibly say that we did not love their house and want to buy it. But I could credibly say that there were other properties we would also settle for.

9. Don't Assume That Others Will Be Rational

As we saw in the case with the seller's corporate apartment, people do not always react rationally. There may be individual biases or things that are important to them that make no sense to you. You also don't know the seller's position in many cases. Do they really need to sell? Are there any other parties still looking? How much time do they have to sell? Their reactions to individual issues will be highly influenced by such subjective factors that are hard to uncover.

Understanding the motivations of your counterparty become even harder in a cross-border deal. Although you need to be careful with generalizations, Americans tend to be more aggressive and extroverted in negotiations. But some of the quieter, more thoughtful negotiators from Asia have been the hardest that I have ever dealt with. Their quietness and depth of thought can make it very hard to determine what is most important to them. You can't assume that they value and approach things in the exact same way as people from your home country. Being able to adapt to the style of your counterparty is absolutely critical for effective negotiating.

10. Prepare, Prepare, Prepare

I continue to be amazed how many people will come to a multimillion-dollar negotiation without having done their homework. To be most effective, you should have a list of points that are critical to you (i.e., the ones you need to win). You should prepare a second list of points you would really like to win, but you could give in on if you have to. The third list is points that you feel may be important to the other side, but that are not critical to you (i.e., the "trade-bait" list). Once you enter the negotiation and observe the approach of the other side, you can determine how to handle each one of these lists.

As stated earlier, the toughest negotiations are those when the other side's critical issues are the same as yours. This makes a collaborative negotiation very hard. By definition, in order for the deal to get done, each side will have to give in on issues that they really hate to give in on. Alternatively, if there is not much overlap between the other party's priorities and yours, it can be a much more effective negotiation, making both parties reasonably happy.

While every deal is different, I have found that purchase price is a critical area to both sides in almost every M&A negotiation that I have encountered. This makes proper preparation doubly important. You need to think about the "non-price" things you are willing to give up in order to maximize value. For example, is the industry of the target company environmentally sensitive? If not, perhaps you could live with a weak environmental indemnity for the seller if, in exchange for that, you could lower the purchase price by 5 percent. Only by preparing, knowing what your needs are, and anticipating the needs of the seller can you manage the most effective negotiations.

CHAPTER 9

Making It Right

Don't confuse fame with success. Madonna is one, Helen Keller is the other.

—Erma Bombeck

On November 15, 2010, Caterpillar announced its plan to buy Wisconsin-based Bucyrus International. Bucyrus, a 131-year-old production company specializing in mining equipment, produced machinery that dwarfed the equivalent made by Caterpillar. Bucyrus's largest shovel could fill in three scoops what Caterpillar's largest truck could carry, 720,000 pounds of rock. Before the deal, Caterpillar could sell mine operators 30 percent of the mobile equipment they needed, but with Bucyrus, Caterpillar could now sell them 70 percent. Investors often dislike big acquisitions, fearing that the buyer must be overpaying. But in this case, Caterpillar's stock immediately went up after the deal was announced, indicating shareholders agreed that buying Bucyrus was a great idea.

So far in this book we have reviewed many examples of deals that ended up in disaster. And hopefully we have learned lessons about the common pitfalls to avoid in M&A. But what was different about the Caterpillar Bucyrus deal? Why did it work? The answers lay in a deeper analysis of the deal, the motivations of management, and the techniques used to analyze and integrate the company.

BACKGROUND

In April 2011, Caterpillar announced first-quarter profits exceeding Wall Street's expectations that pushed the stock to an all-time high, 30 percent above its previous peak. Profits for the year were 10 percent higher than the previous record set in 2008. Caterpillar dealers told Wells Fargo analyst Andrew Casey that demand was so strong that "Caterpillar could sell anything it produces." It seemed that the company could do no wrong.

The financial crisis and recession significantly impacted almost every company across the globe. While the recession clearly hit Caterpillar as well, they weathered the storm better than most. This is because Caterpillar had carefully planned for the downturn long before it happened. When most competitors were starting to develop countermeasures for the crisis, Caterpillar had long since begun implementing its contingency plans.

To understand why Caterpillar was in a position to react immediately to the recession, one needs to understand the cyclical nature of the firm's business. Caterpillar machines were expensive investments that lasted for decades. So, you might think that sales would always track closely the over-all GDP growth of the economy. But in reality Caterpillar's sales varied wildly. When the economy was strong, customers always found the money for new, cutting-edge earthmovers. But when corporate budgets tightened, the multi-decade longevity of Caterpillar's machines actually served to eco-nomically harm the company. It was easy for a customer to put off buying a new excavator in a downturn because they would last forever if maintained properly. Further, many cash-strapped owners would flood the market with used machines that had lots of life left in them. These two things combined to depress sales of new equipment when the economy slowed.

Given the historically volatile movement in sales, Caterpillar did two things to guard itself against a downturn. First, even during good economic times, the firm was planning for a downturn. The managers of each unit were forced to model the worst trough in their history. Caterpillar's CEO, Doug Oberhelman, said, "Let's say you're running mining, and sales drop 80 percent in two years, how are you going to react to make money? Well, you can imagine how popular that was in 2005. Nobody wanted to talk about it. But we forced them through the exercise."

Second, management requested a forward-looking view of the economy, realizing the company's susceptibility to GDP shifts. To do so, management had once asked Caterpillar's economists to find a leading indicator that pre-dicted these shifts in U.S. GDP. This indicator turned out to be the company's sales to the number of users. Using this metric, Caterpillar anticipated the U.S. recession coming in the third quarter of 2007 and said so publicly, trig-gering a 2.6 percent one-day drop in the S&P 500.

The ability to predict the recession (although not its depth!), the imple-mentation of the contingency plans, and a thorough long-term strategy resulted in Caterpillar's performance exceeding that of its peers throughout the recession. By 2010 the firm had enough resources not only to make it out of the recession unscathed, but to spend the $8.6 billion required to buy Bucyrus International. By analyzing Caterpillar's acquisition of Bucyrus in more detail, we can learn several key lessons on how management can increase their chances of doing a good deal versus the failures that happen so frequently.

BE STRATEGIC

Caterpillar was very thoughtful about the financial outlook and how their business would be influenced if the economy took a downtown. They spent time in advance thinking about the types of companies and industries they would buy into versus just pursuing the first deal that came along.

Management would drill down from the high-level strategic analysis to find companies that met their parameters and then pursue those that were available in this space. The company would pass on companies that did not fit into one of their broader industry or geographic focus areas. This *strategic* approach to M&A can drive very good results if executed properly.

Some companies fall into the trap of being too optimistic, only pursuing opportunities that they see and are readily available. This is called an *opportunistic* approach to M&A. Management teams following this approach would argue it is more efficient. Why bother looking at a number of companies that may not even be for sale? By concentrating only on those for sale, a company's limited M&A resources can be directed most efficiently. While both opportunistic and strategic approaches can produce good results, the evidence would indicate that deals that have the strategic thought behind them tend to be more successful than those that are purely opportunistic.

Early in my career, I worked for a Fortune 500 company providing security services throughout North America. An opportunity came up to purchase a smaller security operation located in Sweden. I was sent to complete due diligence on the company, assess the opportunity, and determine whether we should pursue it. As happens in many deals, a level of excitement grew around the transaction. Many people at my company wanted the deal to happen, and I certainly did as well. I was finally leading my own due diligence and, better yet, it was an interesting overseas deal. I was quite happy with myself.

Unfortunately, this enthusiasm skewed my judgment. The target was a sound company with a strong management team and a good local reputation. I spent a week in Sweden getting to know the business and the team better. There were certainly positive aspects to the deal. But the business had several serious issues with its customer base and projected revenue streams. Its product was becoming less competitive. Several large customers had recently left, and sales margins were under pressure.

As I boarded the plane back to New York, I tried to convince myself that we should pursue this transaction despite all of these issues. I had just spent a lot of time and money traveling to review this exciting new venture. Would I be viewed as a failure if I did not "come home with the deal"? Certainly there were some legitimate reasons to proceed with the deal. Further, it was available immediately and could help our company expand into Europe and grow. It was a good price, and we had the inside track to win it.

But when I returned to the office, my boss asked me to outline the strategic rationale for buying this Swedish business. I tried to make a case based on the quality of the management team, the brand name, the historical financial results, and so forth. But he was asking a different question. He was asking me whether I had considered this deal in the context of our company's overall strategy and goals, not whether it was a good opportunistic play. What were the pros and cons of our company even being located in Sweden? Did our company even want to be global versus focusing on the current North American operations? Did we investigate other firms in Sweden that might be available for sale if we had only asked the question? Not only should I have had the answers when I returned, these fundamental questions should have been answered before I even started spending money on travel to Sweden for due diligence.

Contrast this with the experience of Caterpillar. Caterpillar management had taken a longer-term view on the economy and their strategy. They focused on the industries and core competencies that they would need in order to compete in a more difficult economy. They had a long-term strategy for their company and used strategic acquisitions to deliver it. When a specific opportunity arose, management were ready to act on it because they had done their homework. They did not merely react to each opportunistic acquisition that came along.

There is a certain amount of opportunism in any acquisition; obviously you can only buy what is for sale. It can be very tempting to pursue a target company that may add short-term financial benefit, even if there is no strategic rationale. It is easy to get hyped up around a deal and lose your perspective. However, a disciplined approach from the top down will help you better screen opportunities and focus your M&A team on only those acquisitions that will not only add financial benefits, but also aid the strategic, long-term value to your firm.

MAINTAIN A RATIONAL ORGANIZATIONAL STRUCTURE

Caterpillar is a good example of putting a rational organizational structure around a deal to maximize its chance of success.[1] Throughout the deal, Caterpillar Group President Steve Wunning maintained executive office accountability for Caterpillar's Global Mining business, including the Bucyrus addition. In other words, the ultimate responsibility for the success of the deal rested with the president. However, under this level the business was grouped into three divisions run by a mixture of Caterpillar and Bucyrus executives reporting directly to Wunning:

1. Dave Bozeman, from Caterpillar, led the Integrated Manufacturing Operations Division, which included the global manufacturing operations for Caterpillar mining products. The division had manufacturing operations in Asia, Australia, Europe, and North America.

2. Chris Curfman, from Caterpillar, led the Mining Sales and Marketing Division, with global responsibility for maintaining and enhancing customer relationships, developing the global marketing strategy, and ensuring future growth opportunities.
3. Luis de Leon, previously chief operating officer for Bucyrus, was elected by the Caterpillar board of directors to lead the new Mining Products Division. The division was responsible for overall mining product strategy development, product design, and product sourcing.

Including representatives from the buyer and the target in senior roles after an acquisition helped to solidify employees of both parties and make sure that the voices of both sides are heard. An acquisition can be stressful. The target's executives can be very helpful in senior management roles to assist in the integration and help the employees of the target to embrace their new owner. At the same time, the buyer should maintain a majority of these roles, reflecting their new ownership and ultimate accountability for running the company. The buyer needs to take feedback from the target company management, but they must assume responsibility for the combined operations. Finding the right balance between being collegiate with target management while still having control of the new entity is a key competency of successful buyers.

Finally, it is helpful for buyers to have a small core team of experienced dealmakers who know the process and can help with the details of a transition plan. Simple things like getting the accounting systems of buyer and seller to talk to each other are much easier with people from both sides of the new business to coordinate. They know the players, have preexisting relationships with the functional areas, and can bring in experts from the business units, IT, HR, sales functions, and external resources, such as tax and legal specialists where necessary.

STRUCTURE THE DEAL PROPERLY

Caterpillar bought Bucyrus through a form of transaction known as a "stock purchase." In a stock deal, Caterpillar essentially purchased all of the outstanding shares of Bucyrus stock to obtain 100 percent control. Another purchase method could have been an "asset purchase." In an asset purchase, the buyer takes specific title to the assets of the target company. The buyer still owns the majority of the target company, but they do it by buying specific assets rather than the stock issued to support and value these assets.

The advantages of stock purchase to Caterpillar are as follows:

- Most of the buyer's contracts will carry over to the seller and will not need to be renegotiated, unless they contain a "change in control" clause. This clause, if present, protects vendors, customers, and other third parties from doing business with the new entity if they decide not to. For example, a major customer could cancel a long-term order for equipment because they had contracted for it with Bucyrus before the merger, and Caterpillar was now the counterparty. This can present material exposure for any buyer and has to be investigated as part of the due-diligence process.
- There are no transfer taxes as the assets do not need to be retitled in a new buyer's name; they are automatically transferred through the value of the stock. You see this phenomenon in the airline industry where airlines generally merge or buy fleets of planes under stock deals. If not, an asset deal would require the buyer to physically ground the planes for a time to change the title, registration, asset tag, and so forth. This inconvenience and cost can be avoided in a properly structured stock deal.
- Many target companies have large net operating loss carryforwards (NOLs) that can help reduce the amount of taxes paid going forward. Under a stock deal, NOLs can be preserved and offset to income generated by the buyer post-closing.

The disadvantages of stock purchase are:

- The buyer avoids paying taxes on the stock transfer, but the buyer does have to pay taxes on the difference between the sales proceeds and the tax basis in the assets sold. For companies with a long tenure, this can create a material tax charge for the seller.
- Employment and union agreements will carry over to the buyer automatically if no change of control is present. While this could be viewed as a positive, it does make it difficult and/or expensive to reduce operating costs after an acquisition is completed.
- The buyer has a lower tax basis in the target company and less value to take as a depreciation write-off against future tax liabilities.

RECOGNIZE THE IMPORTANCE OF BRAND

The tendency of the buyer in many deals might be to rebrand the new company, change logos, implement strategy, change tag lines, and so on to make them consistent with that of the buyer immediately after closing the deal.

However, when this deal was announced, Bucyrus felt strongly that they should retain their company brand.[2] Caterpillar decided to maintain the Bucyrus name for a defined period of time with a gradual process toward the Caterpillar branding for all equipment. Balancing the immediate desire for change with legitimate sensitivities of the company being bought is key to any deal.

Another example of this approach was Lenovo's acquisition of IBM's personal computer division in 2005 and the Think Pad brand name. Speaking about the purchase of IBM's personal computer division, founder of Lenovo, Liu Chuanzhi said,

> *We benefited in three ways from the IBM acquisition. We got the ThinkPad brand, IBM's more advanced PC manufacturing technology and the company's international resources, such as its global sales channels and operation teams. These three elements have shored up our sales revenue in the past several years.*[3]

IBM had spent years building up the reputation and value of the Think Pad brand name. But with effective marketing and product development, Lenovo itself started to be associated with the Think Pad over time. It worked so well that, although Lenovo acquired the right to use the IBM brand name for five years with the acquisition, they only used it for three years. In December 2007, an event called "Lenovo Pride Day" was held. After words of encouragement from management, employees ceremoniously peeled the IBM logos off their Think Pads and replaced them with Lenovo stickers. This is a great example of a transition of a brand name from one company to another in a logical fashion over time.

EFFICIENT DISTRIBUTION

A thoughtful combination of each party's supply and distribution channels is a central part of the merger of any two companies. In this case, the strength of Caterpillar's brand along with its market share relied heavily on Caterpillar's network of dealers who sold CAT equipment. The dealers also provided the majority of post-sales support such as maintenance, spare parts, and servicing. Alternatively, Bucyrus operated a direct sales method; that is, a customer would order a piece of equipment directly from the manufacturer with no dealer in the middle. Following the acquisition, Caterpillar phased out the direct sales model and began to sell the mining equipment through Caterpillar's preexisting dealer network. This approach posed two issues that the firm needed to address.

First, as previously discussed, Bucyrus's equipment was on average much bigger and more expensive than that of Caterpillar. It also sold in lower volumes. This meant that the dealers would potentially need to hold greater amounts of inventory on their balance sheets, expand the size of their facilities, and be more patient in waiting for their stock to be turned into revenue. Second, Bucyrus equipment required a much greater degree of customization than dealers were used to with the standard Caterpillar equipment, vastly adding to the complexity and cost of a typical dealer's activity.

But Caterpillar saw this issue coming and addressed it in the following ways:

- *Factory support.* Application engineers were added to interface directly with customers to provide support for the more complicated equipment.
- *Dealers.* Dealers were trained to be more involved through the entire sales process from sales to post-sales support and maintenance to ensure a positive customer experience end-to-end.
- *Technicians and field staff.* These key individuals, previously employed by Bucyrus, were now employed directly by the equipment dealers to help make the transition to Caterpillar's distribution system more efficient.[4] The approach made sense, as mining equipment requires a lot of replacement parts and post-sales support. It also provided the benefit of reducing direct labor cost by shifting some of the workforce to the dealerships.

Thinking about integration *before* the deal closes is a key to any successful acquisition. Indeed, Caterpillar was very thoughtful in how it would coordinate distribution capabilities with its new company. Making an informed, strong, and clear statement about how things will be organized post-close is critical. People are naturally nervous about their own careers in any acquisition, particularly staff of the target company. Being up front, living up to your word, and having a clear plan of action can make all the difference.

BEWARE OF CULTURE

Understanding and managing the culture of the two entities being combined is a critical element to determining whether mergers and acquisitions succeed or fail. In this deal, the combination of Bucyrus executives with Caterpillar representatives on the management team was a major step toward effectively merging the cultures of each side. We reviewed the impact of company culture on M&A extensively in Chapter 5. This case is a good example of best practice in terms of cultural integration. Caterpillar's thoughtful approach to recognizing that both sides would be going through a difficult transition was key to the short- and long-term success of the deal.

Having thought leaders whom people look up to and who are incentivized to make the combination of companies work can be extraordinarily helpful in allaying the natural fears employees have around job loss, change in strategy, plant closures, and other natural questions in any merger. Respected senior leaders from both sides who appear to be aligned and empowered can be a very calming influence during this difficult integration time.

HAVE FINANCING LINED UP IN ADVANCE

Caterpillar spent a lot of time considering how to finance the deal well in advance of committing to the transaction. At close, J.P. Morgan provided a firm commitment to finance the deal under very tight terms and conditions. This made Caterpillar's bid more competitive because it was not subject to the arrangement of financing and therefore was one less thing to worry about in the critical post-deal period. In addition, by having this approval lined up in advance, Caterpillar was arguably able to negotiate a lower purchase price than if their bid were conditioned on arranging this financing after close. By providing more certainty to the seller, Caterpillar was able to create leverage when negotiating the transaction rather than having to prove they could pay for the deal later.

ESTABLISH AN APPROPRIATE M&A APPROVAL PROCESS

Acquisitive companies should have a quick, fact-based way to make decisions when competing for acquisitions. Establishing a stand-alone M&A committee that controls and steers the flow of deals and makes go/no-go decisions at various points in the process can be very helpful in screening out bad deals early. Letting a bad deal go all the way through execution can obviously have horrible consequences. However, wasting resources on a deal that will never get done is almost as bad. M&A committees can be very helpful in killing bad deals early and redirecting the due diligence resources to other deals that do have a chance of being done. Being responsible around these scarce resources can be a huge benefit to a company's efficiency and culture.

Large, corporate M&A teams can work through deals more quickly with a formalized procedure, but they can sometimes get so focused on finding the next big deal that they lose a clear connection to the strategy of the different business units. The individual business managers impacted by the acquisition should be involved in the process from the start in order to form a view of how to operate the company post-close.

Companies that acquire less may use a leaner, more project-driven approach with less formalized procedures. Often, they forgo an M&A committee and use the standard investment decision-making process instead. This can work well and may even expedite decision making so long as there are few deals, or the deals are small enough that management can address them on a business-unit level. One European consumer company, for example, handles all M&A decisions just as it would other capital expenditure or investment decisions. This ensures that each deal is carefully and critically evaluated on a consistent basis as all such decisions must compete for the same scarce resources.

INTEGRATE EARLY AND OFTEN

Most leadership teams will require some element of formalized integration planning before final deal approval, yet they often fail to provide for any explicit connection between the deal-making process and the target's eventual integration. This disconnect may undermine an acquisition's strategic and operational advantages. All companies, regardless of their approach to M&A, should appoint a clear deal owner, as well as an integration manager who is responsible for providing focused leadership, from well before due diligence until far into the integration effort.

Forcing discussions on integration early in the process is critical to avoid surprises later on. There needs to be a smooth handoff between the deal team closing the transaction and the integration team taking over to run the company post-close. The earlier the integration team can be involved the better. They get to know the target company management, understand the issues of the deal, and are in a much better position to manage the integration having had this context.

CLEAR LEGAL AND REGULATORY PROCESS

The Bucyrus transaction was not subject to heavy regulatory scrutiny by the U.S. regulator, as the combined entity did not pose a threat of monopolizing the market. It was felt that the Bucyrus product would complement and increase Caterpillar's offering in the mining sector. The move was welcomed by Caterpillar Chairman and CEO Doug Oberhelman, who claimed his organization was "very pleased" with the outcome. He reported, "Since we announced our plan to acquire Bucyrus last November, we have continued to hear from our customers that this complementary expansion of our mining product range is what they have been looking for from Caterpillar."[5]

But many acquisitions, especially those in more sensitive industries, can be delayed by months waiting for regulatory approval. National governments are becoming increasingly sensitive to out-of-country buyers looking to get exposure in critical domestic markets like telecom, technology, defense, infrastructure, and classic old brand names. Whether it is concerns around national security or letting valuable domestic brands be taken over by foreign companies, the amount of regulatory oversight is increasing. Buyers need to think through this and develop an approach to getting approval *before* they commit to buy to avoid unnecessary distraction to their core operations.

DON'T OVERPAY

Being disciplined on price is the single most important thing a management team can do to protect their company in an acquisition. Too often, deal teams get caught up in the hype of the deal. They spend months analyzing the target and a lot of money on due diligence, and have often preannounced the deal to investors. At this point there can be a ton of pressure on the team to close the deal, even if they know they are overpaying. Having the discipline to pay only what the target is worth is critical. It is extremely hard to make up for materially overpaying for a property, no matter how well the company is run post-acquisition.

One could argue whether Caterpillar overpaid for this acquisition. On the positive side, the Bucyrus purchase was funded by a mix of cash from the balance sheet and debt provided by banks. No new shares were issued that would have diluted Caterpillar's equity owners at the time. In other words, each share of stock held the same percentage ownership in the company before the transaction as it did after the transaction. There was no need to find new shareholders or to ask existing shareholders for more money to get the deal done. All of this is positive.

On the other hand, one could argue that Caterpillar was not overly disciplined on price. At $7.4 billion, the price was 32 percent more than the market value of Bucyrus stock at time of purchase. It resulted in goodwill of over $3.5 billion at close, representing the excess of the value paid by Caterpillar over the book value of the Bucyrus assets. At the time, this may have made sense given the all-time highs for commodity prices and bullish outlook for developing economies' continued need for raw materials. But when these economies slowed down, commodity prices plunged. In fact, by the third quarter of 2016, analysts started to press for a goodwill write-off on Bucyrus, reflecting the subsequent decline in commodity prices and arguable overpayment for the assets by Caterpillar.

CONTINUOUS LEARNING

The ability to learn from previous deals through a formal education process, such as holding post-deal or post-integration workshops and updated play-books, matters more than the mere experience of doing deals. Indeed, the performance of companies that have a formal post-deal and post-integration learning program is higher, both by qualitative metrics and by total returns to shareholders, than for companies that use an informal post-deal learn-ing process. Yet very few companies have formal learning mechanisms in place.

Project-oriented organizations might hold workshops after each step in the acquisition process in order to develop some degree of continuity among deals by formalizing and documenting what teams have learned and observed along the way. Accountability is another key aspect. For example, General Electric followed a practice of reviewing the financial projections provided to the board to approve a major deal, with the actual results one year later. The deal team and operating management were required to explain all material variances to the plan. This helped to ensure that deal teams provided (1) an honest assessment of projected financial results to the board, as they realized that they would be held accountable for them, and (2) surface areas that consistently worked well, or not so well, so these learnings could be applied to future transactions.

A CASE STUDY: J.P. MORGAN BUYS BEAR STEARNS

In December 2007, Bear Stearns had a growing problem. Credit markets were tightening largely as a result of investment banks' exposure to subprime mortgages. A continually rising housing market drove mortgage lenders to be increasingly aggressive in terms that they offered to subprime borrowers. Bear Stearns was one of the biggest underwriters of complex investments linked to these mortgages. When the housing bubble burst, the value of these securities plummeted overnight.

Bear Stearns' problem started in early 2007, as news about its risky fund-ing spread in the market and its stock price began to fall. By July 2007, two of its hedge funds, heavily invested in subprime mortgages, were liquidated, as investors asked for their money back. In December 2007, Bear Stearns announced the first loss in its 80-year history, resulting from a write-down of $1.9 billion of its mortgage-backed securities.

In March 2008, rumors were circulating in the markets about the financial issues at Bear, and customers began to withdraw funds. By the latter part of the week of March 10, 2008, Bear Stearns hit a liquidity crisis. Bank counterparties to Bear refused to lend them additional money and demanded repayment of Bear's outstanding debt obligations. By the close of business on Friday, March 14, Bear Stearns was about to collapse. Investors were demanding their money back and Bear did not have it. Because it was linked to so many other financial firms, the collapse of Bear threatened not only the investment bank itself, but the entire financial market. The government had to do something to prevent chaos from descending on the United States and in turn the world economy.

U.S. Treasury Secretary Henry Paulson stated that the job of regulators was to address times of turmoil in capital markets, in other words, the exact situation that Bear was currently facing.[6] But the Fed did not want a fire-sale on the assets of Bear Stearns, which would have depressed markets further, so they decided to step in. J.P. Morgan was asked to provide immediate funding for Bear for up to 28 days, with the full support of the U.S. government for this loan. Even with this, Bear's stock had fallen from the previous day's close of $57 per share to $30 per share, close to a 50 percent drop in price in one day.

More had to be done over the weekend to prevent an outright collapse of Bear Stearns. Private equity firms were brought in to look at a sale. However, the only credible bidder to emerge and to have the backing of the Federal Reserve was J.P. Morgan. Bear Stearns had to prepare for two potential outcomes: (1) a sale to J.P. Morgan by Monday morning, or (2) an immediate bankruptcy filing. After over 80 years, Bear Stearns would no longer be an independent financial institution one way or another.

On Monday morning, it was announced that J.P. Morgan, with specific backing from the U.S. government, would acquire Bear Stearns for $2 per share. Jamie Dimon, CEO of J.P. Morgan, argued that they did not have sufficient time to perform due diligence between Friday night and Monday morning and needed some protection for things they may have missed in the books of Bear Stearns. As a result, they convinced the government to provide up to $30 billion in guarantees for any bad assets they purchased that Monday that ultimately proved to be uncollectable.

The stockholders of Bear Stearns were furious. Certainly the venerable firm was worth more than $2 per share. This price was a 93 percent discount to the $30 closing price from Friday night. To make matters worse, the stock had traded as high as $150 per share in mid-2007. Unsurprisingly, multiple suits were filed against the merger, arguing that the Bear Stearns board of directors had not protected shareholder rights in accepting the bid of $2 per share.

In response to public backlash, on March 24, 2008, J.P. Morgan amended the merger agreement to provide $10 per share of stock, increasing the total value of the deal to $1.2 billion. Although still massively below recent stock highs, this did seem to appease shareholders a bit.

So what did Jamie Dimon and J.P. Morgan do right on this deal? First, they did not rush into a deal they were not ready to commit to. J.P. Morgan realized that there was no way to complete due diligence on a multibillion-dollar global company between Friday night and Monday morning. They pressed for a guarantee from the government to protect against issues missed in the abbreviated diligence process. And when they did not get it, they refused to walk into a deal that did not make sense for the shareholders of J.P. Morgan.

Second, they paid a good price. They were not pressured into overbidding for a damaged property. In fact, they received such a good deal at $2 per share that they later agreed to raise it, even though they had no legal obligation to do so. Of course, public perception did have something to do with J.P. Morgan's agreement to raise this price. But the deal still made imminent sense at $10 per share. Rather than endure the public backlash for "stealing" the company, J.P. Morgan agreed to a bid that worked for Bear Stearns' shareholders while still providing outstanding returns for J.P. Morgan on the transaction.

Jamie Dimon stated, "We believe the amended terms are fair to all sides and reflect the value and risks of the Bear Stearns franchise, and bring more certainty for our respective shareholders, clients, and the marketplace. We look forward to a prompt closing and being able to operate as one company."

Alan Shwartz, president and CEO of Bear Stearns, issued the following statement:

> *Our Board of Directors believes that the amended terms provide both significantly greater value to our shareholders, many of whom are Bear Stearns employees, and enhances our coverage and certainty for our customers, counterparties and lenders. The substantial share issuance to J.P. Morgan Chase was a necessary condition to obtain a full set of amended terms, which in turn, were essential to maintaining Bear Stearns' financial stability. The past week has been an incredibly difficult time for Bear Stearns. This transaction represents the best outcome based upon the current circumstances.*

Bear Stearns prided itself on never being considered a white-shoe Wall Street firm, and often operated on the edge of the industry. With an 80-year history it must have been incredibly difficult for Schwartz and his management team to cede control to a rival bank. This shows the desperate situation that Bear Stearns and its board were faced with that weekend.

Jamie Dimon and his team knew they had all the leverage. They cut a deal that was massively accretive to J.P. Morgan's share price while still looking like the white knight that averted potentially disastrous consequences for the entire U.S. economy. They integrated the business quickly and were very direct with Bear Stearns employees. They immediately took control of Bear's soaring headquarters on Madison Avenue. They agreed to guarantee withdrawals from worried creditors of the bank. They rebranded Bear Stearns as J.P. Morgan quickly and efficiently. There was no doubt in anyone's mind about who was running the show after this acquisition.

Only 12 months later, the combined company looked very different:[7]

- Of the 14,000 Bear Stearns employees as of March 2008, only 5,000 remained at J.P. Morgan as of March 2009.
- One of the few operations that kept its name was Bear Stearns Private Client Services, a brokerage and trading business.
- Bear Stearns' Alan "Ace" Greenberg, former CEO and chairman of the board from 1985 to 2001, was forced to work for J.P. Morgan as vice chairman of Bear Stearns' Retail Business at J.P. Morgan Chase.
- All Bear Stearns signs at the former headquarters were immediately removed and replaced with J.P. Morgan signs.
- J.P. Morgan's culture superseded the very different culture at Bear Stearns. Bear Stearns workers were accustomed to a casual workplace with lots of freedom, and they resisted the more formalized procedures at J.P. Morgan, including performance reviews, detailed operating memos, and many additional, formal meetings.
- The situation with J.P. Morgan and Bear Stearns was very different from the Caterpillar Bucyrus integration. In the Bucyrus deal, representatives from each company were put in senior management roles with gradual integration and a melding of the best of each side's cultures in the newly merged company. But in the case of Bear Stearns, J.P. Morgan took immediate control, imposing their culture and way of doing business on Bear Stearns from the start. But each form of integration was suitable in relation to the needs of each particular situation. In the case of Bear Stearns:
  - This was a distressing event where Bear would not have survived had a larger company with large financial backing not swooped in, purchased, and integrated them swiftly.

- This was Wall Street, where each bank had a strong, contradictory culture and had historically engaged in fierce competition with one another. Melding the cultures would have taken a long time and probably never have worked.
- The companies needed to be integrated quickly to prevent financial disaster for Bear Stearns and the U.S. economy at large. J.P. Morgan did not have the luxury of an extended due-diligence time frame.
- Each company had very strongminded CEOs. It needed to be clear that J.P. Morgan had the upper hand and would be the surviving organization after the bailout. Strong statements to this effect included the rebranding of Bear Stearns to J.P. Morgan quickly and the relocation of Bear Stearns' corporate headquarters. Both elements made it explicitly clear who was in charge.

The contrast between Caterpillar's purchase of Bucyrus and J.P. Morgan's purchase of Bear Stearns is a terrific example of two very different success stories of companies adapting the integration process to the situation at hand. In Caterpillar's case it was the combination of two industrial firms with different cultures but with the same ambitions in a marketplace. Caterpillar could afford a gradual integration process with representatives of each side involved in the merger of the two firms to take the best practices of each.

In the case of Bear Stearns, the combination of two firms that had been massively competitive throughout history resulted in the insolvency of one firm to the advantage of the other. Bear Stearns had taken imprudent risks and suffered the consequences. A quick and powerful integration made perfect sense, so J.P. Morgan imposed their brand name and style of doing business into a situation that needed immediate attention.

CONCLUSION

So what does it take to do a good deal? Although we have outlined some general principles, it really depends on the circumstances at the time. The Caterpillar Bucyrus transaction could not be more different from the J.P. Morgan Bear Stearns purchase. But they both worked in their own way. The ability to adapt the processes and procedures discussed in this book to the situation in hand is absolutely critical. Having the perspective to make these difficult choices will determine ultimate success or failure in mergers and acquisitions you and your firm decide to pursue.

NOTES

1. Caterpillar News, "Caterpillar Completes Acquisition of Bucyrus," 2001, http://www.prnewswire.com/news-releases/caterpillar-completes-acquisition-of -bucyrus-creating-mining-equipment-group-with-unmatched-product-range-and -unrivaled-customer-support-125214769.html.
2. http://www.bizjounrals.com, 2010.
3. Steve Hamm, *The Race for Perfect: Inside the Quest to Design the Ultimate Portable Computer* (New York: McGraw-Hill), 2008.
4. Caterpillar, Q2 2011 Caterpillar Inc. Earnings and Bucyrus Acquisition conference call (7/22/2011), final transcript.
5. The Gap Partnership, "Sales Negotiation Trading May Aid CapitalSource," 2010, http://egap.thegappartnership.com/negotiation-news/2011/january/sales -negotiation-training-may-aid-capitalsource.aspx.
6. Treasury Secretary Henry M Paulson, Jr. "Remarks on Current Financial and Housing Markets at the U.S. Chamber of Commerce," March 26, 2008.
7. Robin Sidel and Kate Kelley, "A Year Later: From Fabled to Forgotten," *Wall Street Journal*, March 14 2009.

CHAPTER 10

Where Do We Go from Here?

Some of the best lessons we ever learn are learned from past mistakes. The error of the past is the wisdom and success of the future.

—Dale Turner, American musician

HOW FAST WE FORGET

Toward the end of the 2007–2008 financial crisis, many pundits proclaimed that we had finally learned our lesson and we would never go back to the crazy days of the heated economy that immediately preceded, and arguably caused, the market crash. Market experts were sure that we would be more careful from now on. We would no longer leverage up our homes. We would pay off personal debt on time. And we would encourage corporate executives to be more conservative in their approach to business.

But look at what is happening in our economy less than ten years later. Despite increasing geopolitical and business risk, interest rates remain near the lowest levels in history. The cost, availability, and terms on debt are as friendly to borrowers as ever. Consumers are starting to lever up again. In May 2017, total U.S. credit card debt passed the $1 trillion dollar level for the first time in history. Yet the equity markets continue to perform as if nothing has changed. By the middle of 2017 the Dow Jones Industrial Average had closed over 20,000 for the first time in history. There was an ever-increasing gap between the amount of risk inherent in the global economy and the inflated asset values that did not reflect this level of risk. In this final chapter, we will discuss the impact that these and other current trends will likely have on M&A in the coming years.

In an interesting article written by Rob Marstand in *Seeking Alpha*[1] he identified "debt zombies" as those companies trading on a stock market whose annual profit does not cover the amount of their debt payments each year, let alone the money needed to cover other corporate expenses. The number of these zombie companies went from 5.5 percent of all listed companies pre-crisis (2006) to 8 percent post-crisis in 2011, and they have been growing since then. As early as the end of 2015, the percentage of debt zombie companies increased to 10.5 percent, almost double the levels immediately prior to the financial crisis.

In addition, the protections in these debt agreements are becoming more and more relaxed, making it harder for lenders to collect their proceeds, especially if we run into problems anything like we did in 2007. Let's take one simple example of a pre-crisis debt instrument called the "PIK toggle note." In this form of debt, the borrower does not have to pay back any current interest or principal if either (1) they don't have enough cash to make a payment, or (2) they have enough cash to pay but simply don't want to. Any unpaid portions add to the total amount owed at debt maturity.

Think about this. You are a bank who just lent a company, say $10 million. You have no ability to demand your money back regardless of how the borrower is performing. Even if the borrower's revenues collapse, a major disaster hits, or corporate cash is running out, there is nothing you can do to force repayment. To make matters worse, the amount of your debt keeps going up as interest payments are deferred. This type of debt instrument, and others like it, were the first to fail in the Great Recession. When cash is tight, borrowers will make only the payments they are legally required to make. In a PIK toggle note there is no requirement and, by the time the note becomes due, no cash to pay back the borrower.

A third and final example can be seen in the releveraging of personal homeownership over the past several years. Economists universally agree that one primary cause of the recession was a bubble in the housing market and people using these inflated values to take on more debt. When the market crashed and home values came down, consumers became cash constrained and could not continue making mortgage payments. When banks forced them to sell their homes, they were "upside-down" (i.e., the amount of loan owed was larger than the market value of the home). This resulted in a cycle of foreclosures and stressed sales, driving the housing market down even more.

Well, those days may be back. The median sales price for existing homes rose to an all-time high of $263,800 in June 2017, up 40 percent from the beginning of 2014, according to the National Associate of Realtors. Consumers are once again using these inflated values as their "piggy bank" to lever up their home via home equity lines, take out money, and spend it on other areas. In the second quarter of 2017, home equity lines increased by 8 percent to almost $46 billion, their highest level since 2008 as reported by Equifax.[2] This is yet another example of how short people's memories are.

We could go on and on about the seemingly counterintuitive situation in which we find ourselves in the current economy with both debt levels and asset values near all-time highs, but at an extremely uncertain time in the world. At some point this trend will surely put pressure on M&A markets. We have tried to show in this book that while a well-thought-out and properly structured acquisition can indeed accelerate a company's growth, there are certain common errors that have happened time and time again. We intentionally included deals from over a decade old to current transactions to show that the impact of these errors can be dramatic regardless of the current economic environment.

A volatile economy leaves even less room for errors in execution and puts more pressure on trying to avoid these pitfalls in M&A. Going forward, deal teams need to be cognizant of both this current uncertainty and the root causes of historic failure. History has shown that we are not very good at forecasting the future. Whether you like him or not, who would have thought five years ago that in 2017 Donald Trump would be president of the United States? Who would have predicted that a majority of U.K. citizens would vote to exit the European Union? Nevertheless, how we approach mergers and acquisitions should be influenced by the past and also by our best guess of what will happen going forward.

I recently taught a group of mid-career students a course in financial strategy at a major university MBA program. After spending a day in class on the topic of private equity, one student asked the inevitable question, "Will this material be on the final exam?" After dodging the question, I related to students that ten years from now, they would likely not remember much of what I taught them in an eight-week class. But if I could leave students with three to five concepts that they would remember and apply to their career or personal life 5, 10, and 15 years from now, then I had done my job. Hopefully I have provided the reader with a similar perspective from this book. I would like to end with what I see as the seven most relevant trends going forward that will have the biggest impact on M&A over the next three to five years.

1. Increasing Pressure from Multiple Constituencies

In August 1981, then-CEO of General Electric, Jack Welsh, stated, "GE's vision is to be the biggest or second biggest market player and to return maximum value to shareholders." In fact, almost all public companies at the time were focused on driving value for this "most important" stakeholder. After all, it was the shareholders who entrusted their own savings to the management team to invest it in company operations, to pay dividends, and ultimately to return proceeds significantly higher than their initial investment. So what were the relevant metrics? Stock price, cash flow, earnings per share, quarterly earnings, and dividends all became the metrics management sought to maximize. People had invested in GE shares, and management's duty was to drive that share price, and investor returns, as high as possible.

Credit to GE and to Jack Welsh that over its 100-plus-year history GE has always been willing to reconsider its positions and adapt as the environment changed. Over time, other stakeholders such as employees, the community, regulators, customers, and the environment became more important constituencies that CEOs needed to address. So by March 2009,

Welsh stated, "On the face of it, shareholder value is the dumbest idea in the world. Shareholder value is a result, not a strategy... your main constituencies are your employees, your customers, and your products." This was an interesting new lens to view not only how you run a company, but how you approach an acquisition.

The world has evolved to a place where other critical things like the environment, regulators, employees, and local communities can have a material impact on a company's cash flow, earnings per share, or stock price and ultimately shareholder value. Not only is focusing on things like a safe environment and taking care of your employees the right thing to do; the long-term value of your company will be materially impacted by how effectively you address them.

One particularly difficult example was the explosion of the BP Deepwater Horizon on April 20, 2010, causing the release of 4.9 billion barrels of oil into the Gulf of Mexico. Consider the following constituencies that then-CEO of BP, Tony Hayward, had to face that day:

- *Employees.* Eleven crew members died on the offshore platform that day.
- *Environment.* Eleven hundred miles of coastal wetlands were contaminated with 32 national wildlife areas impacted.
- *Community.* Commercial fishing production dropped by 20 percent, and the Gulf of Mexico rental reservations fell by over 25 percent in the year after the spill.
- *Shareholders.* While still not fully settled, BP estimates that the total penalties, fines, settlements with state and local authorities, and so on will add up to over $60 billion! While it has recovered somewhat since, BP's share price dropped by $70.3 billion or 59 percent in the hundred days following this disaster.

This event is clearly one of the most dramatic ever, but CEOs and boards face smaller struggles with a wide variety of constituencies every day.

To make it even harder, the interests of many different constituencies may not be perfectly aligned. Trying to make a decision that aligns the interests of each can be quite difficult. Balancing such things as fair pay and compensation for all employees while maintaining a conservative financial position and consistent company profitability for shareholders is important. The balance between the cost and need for regulatory compliance while remaining competitive in the market, along with dealing with other important constituencies, are beyond the scope of this book. But we can be sure that these will continue to be areas that drive a CEO's approach to her business and the M&A strategy used to support the company's objectives.

2. Activist Shareholders

There has been, and will continue to be, increasing influence placed on CEOs and boards of public companies by activist shareholders who take a material position in the company's stock. Most activists argue that, by virtue of their large investment in the company, they have the right to be consulted on major decisions facing management either informally or through a formal role on the company's board of directors. In recent years, activists have started to weigh in on topics such as overall company strategy, the composition of board, the proper CEO, dividend policy, and even the company's M&A strategy.

In 2017, a U.S. hedge fund called Elliott Management Company accumulated a 9.5 percent position in Dutch paints group Akzo Nobel. Despite this material economic interest, Elliott was unable convince the board of Akzo to agree to a $27 billion takeover by U.S. paint provider PPG. The hedge fund believed that at this value, it made sense for the company to be acquired rather than continue its long-term growth strategy. Skeptics argued that Elliot only wanted to move forward because they would receive an immediate material gain on their Akzo investment. This is a frequent criticism of activist investors, that their time horizon is very short and not in alignment with other shareholders in the company, management, or the board.

In this case, management was successful in fending off PPG's unsolicited offer, supported by Elliott and several other shareholders, to buy the entire company. But there were consequences. Litigation quickly ensued. Dissident shareholders, including Elliott, called for the Akzo chairman to resign. To quell the distraction management ultimately agreed to sell its chemicals unit, use a portion of the sales proceeds to pay out up €1.6 billion in dividends to shareholders, change out the CEO, and make several changes to the company's supervisory board.

This case presents a good illustration of the increasing influence larger shareholders are demanding in governing a company. Mergers and acquisitions are normally quite material events that activist shareholders will want a say on. CEOs can no longer assume that all constituencies will simply go along with their buyout plans, or alternatively with their response to offers to being bought. The influence of activist shareholders will continue to increase and will have to be considered in the M&A landscape in the years to come.

3. Trend from Conglomerates to Pure Play

A *conglomerate* is a single company involved in a wide variety of industries and product lines at the same time. The longstanding Fortune 500 company

Johnson & Johnson headquartered in New Jersey is a good example of a conglomerate. J&J has divisions and product lines focused on everything from consumer healthcare to medical devices to pharmaceuticals. The most popular argument in favor of conglomerates is the diversification they provide in one stock. By owning different products in different countries, a conglomerate is not exposed to any one economy or industry decline. For example, if the Neutrogena Skin Products division of J&J is not doing well, perhaps the Life Sciences Blood Glucose Machine product line is expanding. These products focus on very different needs of people, and their performance is likely not closely correlated, mitigating the risk to isolated market disruptions.

A conglomerate also presents management with an opportunity to take advantage of synergies between divisions. The Baby Care division of J&J likely has some similar customers or technology with the Skin and Hair Care division. By marketing to one set of customers, J&J will likely reach customers of these adjacent product lines as well to get more out of each advertising dollar spent. Technology around production methods can be shared between product lines to lower cost. Economies of scale can be realized by driving corporate skillsets around purchasing, technology, tax planning, or human resource policies across the different divisions with very little incremental cost. Finally, the J&J brand name has significant messaging value that can be spread among multiple product lines to provide instant credibility to sub-brands like Band-Aid and Tylenol.

However, as financial markets have matured, the ability to diversify one's investment portfolio has become much easier and less expensive. Investors can now diversify industry risk themselves by putting together a portfolio of pure-play companies from different industries. Facebook would be a good example of a pure-play company. At least for now, the Facebook product lines remain pretty much focused around some aspect of social media. Alternatively, a conglomerate like Google, which started off as a search engine company, has diversified into so many new industries that it ultimately created a new stock (Alphabet) to house this wide variety of focus areas.

There are several arguments in favor of pure-play companies and against conglomerates. One of the strongest is the distraction that managing a complex conglomerate can cause to a management team. The argument goes: How could a typical CEO or board make informed decisions ranging from whether to invest in a search engine technology one day, to starting a self-driving car division the next, to a large insurance acquisition the following day? Over the past decade, businesses, technology, and product lines have become more complex, requiring more specialized skillsets to adequately evaluate each. Finding a CEO who is an expert on multiple industries along with having the leadership and business acumen to execute an overall company strategy is very difficult, indeed.

A related argument is that conglomerate stocks are generally undervalued because stock analysts have trouble understanding multiple complex
industries as well. This results in the "sum of the parts" valuation inevitably
being less than the value of each independent unit put together. Why bother
with the complexity, corporate overhead, and valuation issues of a conglomerate when sophisticated financial markets now allow investors to create
their own industry portfolio through a combination of discrete pure-play
investments?

Either side of this equation could be argued as there are numerous
examples of successful conglomerates as well as pure-play companies.
Rather, my point is that the current trend toward pure plays may be
one of the few things that dampens M&A activity in the coming years.
From a corporate perspective, conglomerates have historically been heavy
buyers, using acquisitions to expand into new markets and industries. If
conglomerates fall out of favor, management teams will be less inclined to
use M&A to expand and instead focus on their core industries. However,
the current trend toward pure plays could stimulate the divestment activities
of multiproduct global players like Akzo, where the activist shareholder
influenced management to dispose of non-core operations.

4. Increasing Nationalism Around Cross-Border Deals

The Kraft Cadbury merger we discussed in Chapter 6 was one of the first
deals where a sense of nationalism in cross-border M&A started to surface.
The venerable British confectionary institution started by John Cadbury in
1824 was to be taken over by the large U.S. conglomerate, Kraft. Although
the deal ultimately closed, there were considerable concerns both before and
after the deal from the British that they should not let one of the most treasured British companies of all time fall into U.S. hands. It is also a good
example of the difficulty in managing multiple constituencies. Kraft was
heavily criticized after the deal closed for a decision to shut down a large
plant in Somerdale, U.K., which resulted in the elimination of 400 local jobs.
This is a classic example of trying to balance the costs of production, which
might be lower outside of the U.K., to enhance value to one stakeholder
(shareholders), versus the damage it might cause to another stakeholder (the
local community) where Cadbury had maintained a presence for decades.

I fully expect this tension around the foreign purchase of domestic assets
will continue for the foreseeable future. Rightly or wrongly, countries are
becoming more nationalistic and worried about what happens within their
borders. Germany is another example of a country becoming more sensitive

to foreign takeovers of German assets. In 2016, a $3.5 billion acquisition by a Chinese appliance maker (Midea Group Co.) of the largest robotics maker in Germany (Kuka) stirred national concern about Germany giving away its most advanced technology in exchange for quick cash. More recently, a second deal, Fujian Grand Chips' planned acquisition of Aixtron, a German chipmaker, was delayed after German authorities reopened a regulatory review of the deal due to security concerns around critical technology.

Further reflecting these national concerns, in July 2017 Germany expanded the power of government to unilaterally block foreign takeovers. The government already had the ability to block a company from outside the EU from buying more than 25 percent of a German entity if the deal "endangered public order or national security." But a new directive adopted by the German Cabinet expands these investigation powers to any merger involving "critical infrastructure," including software for power plants, energy, and water supply networks, electronic payments, hospitals, transport systems, advanced defense technology, and surveillance equipment. Brigitte Zypries, German economic minister, indicated that German companies are often forced to compete with businesses in countries that have a "less open economic system than ours" and the expanded rules should "better protect companies involved in critical infrastructure."[3]

I expect this nationalistic pressure to increase not just in Europe, but across North America and Asia. A more politically sensitive environment, expanded interest in mission-critical industries globally, and well-funded corporations and private equity firms will increase the interest and likely the domestic resistance to such major cross-border acquisition proposals.

5. Increased Emphasis on Operating Skills

In any large deal, there are a host of investment bankers, lawyers, consultants, and accountants to maximize value by arranging low-cost financing and developing complex tax structures and long-term strategies to maximize company value. However, while these areas are normally covered in excruciating detail, not enough attention is paid to accumulating the skillsets needed to actually run the company post-closing. The technical experts are very good at what they do, but they generally have never run anything. Operating a large company could not be more different than structuring a typical acquisition. A much different skill set immediately comes into play. Things like leadership, execution, persuasion, and speed take more importance than deal structuring and tax planning once the deal closes.

Many companies have started to focus as much on the post-closing integration as on the pre-close negotiating and structuring. This is critical for an effective acquisition. Too many times the deal person who closed the transaction moves on to the next deal immediately after signing, leaving the poor integration person with a big task he or she may not be prepared for. Having integration people involved from the start of the process so they can get to know the target management team, the issues identified during diligence, and key success factors for the deal is important. Indeed, many of the best buyers of companies today have 100-day acquisition plans, specifically outlining roles, responsibilities, and project milestones post-closing.

The underlying fundamentals indicate that good properties will continue to be more expensive, as there continues to be more demand for target companies than supply. This leaves even less margin for error in operating the company post-close if deal teams expect to achieve their acquisition financial projections. Good buyers have started to recognize this, and people with sound operation skills are becoming more and more important to the M&A industry.

6. Impact of Private Equity on M&A

The rise of the private equity (PE) industry has been the single most fundamental influencer of the M&A market over the past 20 years, and I see no reason for this to change going forward. In a private equity model, investors (called "limited partners," LPs) give their money to the private equity firm (called the "general partner") to invest in a portfolio of companies. Limited partners are typically large pension plans, endowments, or sovereign wealth funds that have excess cash to invest for their constituencies currently but have an obligation to invest this money wisely and pay their members back over the long term.

The PE fund will pool these LP contributions together into a fund structure charging each limited partner 1 to 2 percent of the money they commit as a management fee. They will generally hold the company for three to five years, trying to improve operations, refinance the debt, upgrade management, or expand into new markets. When a company from the portfolio is sold at a gain, the PE firm will typically keep between 10 and 20 percent of the profit over a specified minimum return rate and distribute the excess back to LPs.

This arrangement has worked extraordinarily well over the years, both for the PE firms and for their limited partners. According to Prequin Alternative Asset Research, PE has delivered an average internal rate of return of 8.3 percent to their pension fund investors over the last decade—the best performance of any asset class possible. For the 12 months ended June 30, 2016, Cambridge Associates reported that investors in PE enjoyed a 6 percent internal rate of return compared to just 4 percent returns of the S&P 500. PE firms are happy. They enjoy a 1 percent fee and significant upside given the returns they generate have consistently exceeded the hurdle rate promised to investors. And the LPs are happy. Even after paying large fees to private equity, limited partners are delivering returns better than any other asset class they invest in.

While limited partners continue to invest in other products like the public markets, real estate, venture capital, or fixed income, the attractiveness of private equity is hard to ignore. As a result, the share of pension funds' total available capital allocated to the PE asset class has risen over the years. While it varies by the specific type of limited partner (family office, insurance company, endowment, etc.), generally 5 to 10 percent of their total capital has been allocated to private equity with the amounts continuing to go up each year. And a survey of LPs completed by Prequin in 2016 showed that 92 percent of limited partners planned to maintain or increase their allocation PE going forward.

All of this has resulted in a proliferation in the number PE firms and the amount of capital they manage, called "AUM" (assets under management). By the middle part of 2017, private equity fundraising was at its highest level since the boom years in the run-up to the financial crisis. More than $240 billion was raised across private equity and venture capital funds in North America and Europe during the first seven months of 2017. According to Pitchbook, a data provider, the last time private equity raised this much capital for an equivalent time period was 2007. It brings the total amount of capital available to invest (called "dry powder") in mid-2017 to over $800 billion. Finally according to Prequin, PE firms in total managed over $2.5 trillion in assets.

As mentioned earlier, we have the most liquid debt markets in a long time, at low cost, with relaxed covenants providing PE firms with even more buying power. Dylan Cox, analyst at Pitchbook, stated, "Private Equity and Venture Capital firms continue to enjoy immense success on the fund-raising trail, adding to their already hefty investment sums. Neither asset class shows any sign of slowing down, which could drive valuations higher, leaving deal makers in a precarious position."[4] All of this puts a lot of pressure on PE firms to invest, even if they have to overpay slightly to do it. Limited partners have given the PE firms this money for a reason—to invest it. In fact, LPs are paying 1 to 2 percent of the capital committed as a fee to the PE firm each year. This fee goes away if the PE firm does not spend the money within the three-to-five-year horizon of the fund.

So what can we expect to see going forward as a consequence of all of this?

- *Higher prices for M&A.* According to Bain Consulting, deal values measured as a multiple of the target company cash flow reached 11 times in the latter part of 2016 relative to average multiples of 9 times over the preceding eight years. Clearly the pressure to buy is reaching levels we have not seen since the Great Recession.[5]

- *Larger funds.* The excess capital available from limited partners has already led to more and larger fund sizes. For example, Apollo Global Management raised one single $23.5 billion fund in June 2017.
- *Larger deals.* At the absolute peak of the last M&A cycle, KKR agreed to a $45 billion buyout of TXU, a Texas-based company focused on energy. The company ended up failing, filing for bankruptcy in 2014, and was later sold off in pieces. The PE firms only returned a fraction of the money they invested. While some larger deals have worked very well, the concentration risk in one individual deal like this does increase risk. We have not yet reached the massive deal sizes we saw pre-crisis, but individual deal sizes have been creeping up again. I expect this trend to continue as it is easier to deploy capital faster in larger deals.
- *More firms entering the PE industry.* First-time funds continue to become more popular as many interested pension plans and endowments have been locked out of new funds of the major players due to a lack of supply. Most of the funds raised by established, well-known firms are oversubscribed, meaning that many investors who apply for a piece of the fund don't get it. This forces LPs to look elsewhere to fill their allocation to the private equity asset class. It has allowed some less established, or even first-time, funds that may not have a long investment track record but do have good investor teams who possibly spun out from well-known firms to raise capital.

7. Importance of Deal Skills in Business

The ability to source, negotiate, structure, and integrate mergers and acquisitions has been very important in business and will only continue to become more important going forward. Whether you are sitting on a board reviewing a deal for approval, a CEO developing an M&A strategy, the person doing a deal, or an employee of a target company going through an integration, having a basic knowledge of the principles around M&A is critical. Alternatively, as an investor for an endowment or pension plan, a keen awareness of the M&A market, the drivers to success, and the pitfalls to watch out for can enhance the returns you deliver to your clients.

For reasons outlined previously, M&A will likely grow faster and become even a more integral part of the strategy for public companies, private corporations, and the private equity industry. The management teams of successful acquirers from the deal analyst all the way up to the CEO need to know what questions to ask. These skillsets are increasingly in demand as boards of directors look to upgrade management teams for an increasingly competitive environment in a very uncertain world. For example, the recently announced

CEO of Uber, Dara Khosrowshahi, is known for being a solid dealmaker in M&A. As the previous CEO of Expedia, Khosrowshahi aggressively used M&A to expand into new markets and geographies. This was an important criterion for the top role at Uber, as M&A will likely present an important channel for Uber to access technology while expanding into new product lines and geographies.

In this book we have analyzed mergers and acquisitions ranging from over 20 years ago to those that happened within the past six months. But the themes are largely the same. There have been, and will continue to be, many good deals with very valid reasons to aggressively pursue them. But the M&A field is littered with examples of the same mistakes being repeated time after time. Having an awareness of these key principles and, more importantly, what to do right to secure a positive outcome is critical. Hopefully this book has given the reader an informed overview as well as tangible examples to prove these points.

NOTES

1. "The Debt Zombies Will Overwhelm Us (Again)," by Rob Marstrand, *Seeking Alpha*, August 10, 2017.
2. "Tapping Homes for Cash Is Back," by Christina Rexrode, *Wall Street Journal*, August 28, 2017.
3. "Germany Increases Powers to Block Foreign Takeovers," by Guy Chazan, *Financial Times*, July 13, 2017.
4. As quoted in the *Financial Times*, "Buyout Firms' Fundraising on Track to Reach 10-Year Peak as Targets Dwindle," by Attracta Mooney, August 17, 2017.
5. "Cash Is Piling Up at Buyout Funds," *Wall Street Journal* ("Heard on the Street"), August 28, 2017.

Trinity International/American Public Media Group

Material Adverse Change Clause

"Material Adverse Effect" means a material adverse effect on the Assets taken as a whole; provided the foregoing shall not include any material adverse effect arising out of (i) factors affecting the radio broadcasting industry generally, (ii) general national, regional, or local economic, competitive, or market conditions, (iii) governmental or legislative laws, rules or regulations, or (iv) actions or omissions of Buyer or its Agents.[1]

NOTE

1. Asset Purchase Agreement By and Between Trinity International Foundation and American Public Media Group, September 24, 2007.

Bank of America/Merrill

Material Adverse Change Clause

3.8 Absence of Certain Changes or Events

(a) Since June 27, 2008, no event or events have occurred that have had or would reasonably be expected to have, either individually or in the aggregate, a Material Adverse Effect on the Company. As used in this Agreement, the term "Material Adverse Effect" means, with respect to Parent or Company, as the case may be, a material adverse effect on (i) the financial condition, results of operations or business of such party and its Subsidiaries taken as a whole, provided, however, that, with respect to clause (i), a "Material Adverse Effect" shall not be deemed to include effects to the extent resulting from (A) changes, after the date hereof, in GAAP or regulatory accounting requirements applicable generally to companies in the industries in which such party and its Subsidiaries operate, (B) changes, after the date hereof, in laws, rules, regulations or the interpretation of laws, rules or regulations by Governmental Authorities of general applicability in companies in the industries in which such party and its Subsidiaries operate, (C) actions or omissions taken with the prior written consent of the other party or expressly required by this Agreement, (D) changes in global, national or regional political conditions (including acts of terrorism or war) or general business, economic or market conditions, including changes generally in prevailing interest rates, currency exchange rates, credit markets and price levels or trading volumes in the United States or foreign securities markets, in each case generally affecting the industries in which such party or its Subsidiaries operate and including changes to any previously corrected applied asset marks resulting therefrom, (F) failure in and of itself, to meet earnings projections, but not including any underlying causes thereof, or (G) changes in the trading price of a party's common stock, in and of itself, but not including any underlying causes, except, with respect to clauses (A), (B) and (D), to the extent that the effects of such change are disproportionately adverse to the financial condition, results of operations or business of such party and its Subsidiaries, taken as a whole, as compared to other companies in the industry in which such party and its Subsidiaries operate or (ii) the ability of such party to timely consummate the transactions contemplated by this Agreement.

(b) Since June 27, 2008, through and including the date of this Agreement, Company and its Subsidiaries have carried on their respective businesses in all material respects in the ordinary course of business consistent with their past practice.

(c) Since June 27, 2008, through and including the date of this Agreement, neither Company nor any of its Subsidiaries has (i) except for (A) normal increases for or payments to employees (other than officers subject to the reporting requirements of Section 16(a) of the Exchange Act (the "Executive Officers)) made in the ordinary course of business consistent with past practice of (B) as required by applicable law or contractual obligations existing as of the date hereof, increased the wages, salaries, compensation, pension, or other fringe benefits or perquisites payable to any Executive Officer or other employee or director from the amount thereof in effect as of June 27, 2008, granted any severance or termination pay, entered into any contract to make or grant any severance of termination pay (in each case, except into any contract to make or grant any severance or termination pay (in each case, except as required under the terms of agreements or severance plans listed on Section 3.11 of the Company Disclosure Schedule, as in effect as of the date hereof)), or paid any cash bonus in excess of $1,000,000 other than the customary year-end bonuses in amounts consistent with past practice and other than the monthly incentive payments made to financial advisors under current Company programs, (ii) granted any options to purchase shares of Company Common Stock, any restricted shares of Company Common Stock or any right to acquire any shares of its capital stock, or any right to payment based on the value of Company's capital stock, to any Executive Officer or other employee or director other than grants to employees (other than Executive Officers) made in the ordinary course of business consistent with past practice under the Company Stock Plans or grants relating to shares of Company Common Stock with an aggregate value for all such grants of less than $1 million for any individual, (iii) changed any financial accounting methods, principles or practices of Company or its Subsidiaries affecting its assets, liabilities or businesses, including any reserving, renewal or residual method, practice or policy, (iv) suffered any strike, work stoppage, slow-down, or other labor disturbance, or (v) except for publicly disclosed ordinary dividends on the Company Common Stock or Company Preferred Stock and except for distributions to wholly-owned Subsidiaries of Company to Company or another wholly-owned Subsidiary of Company, made or declared any distribution in cash or kind to its stockholders or repurchased any share of its capital stock or other equity interests.[1]

NOTE

1. Bank of America/Merrill Lynch merger agreement, SEC filings.

About the Author

Bob Stefanowski has 30 years of experience in leading complex global companies and business turnarounds as well as direct investing and service on global boards. Bob was formerly the President and Chief Executive Officer of numerous business units at General Electric and Chief Financial Officer of UBS Investment Bank. He graduated from Fairfield University, has an MBA from Cornell University, a fellowship in finance from UPenn Wharton, and is a former practicing Certified Public Accountant, Chartered Financial Analyst, and Certified Fraud Examiner. He has lectured at leading global universities, including Oxford, Cambridge, and London Business School, and currently serves on the McKinsey & Company Mergers & Acquisitions Advisory Board. Bob is a past participant in the Financial Services Industry Partnership at the World Economic Forum in Davos, Switzerland and was appointed a trustee of the Victoria and Albert Museum by then prime minister of the U.K. Gordon Brown in 2009. Bob lives in Madison, CT, with Amy, his wife of 25 years, and three daughters, Lauren, Rachel, and Megan.

Index

100-Day Plan, usage, 44–45

ABN AMRO, acquisition, 3,
   126–127
   case study, 4–5
Accountability
   culture, 80
   importance, 148
Accounting policies, changes,
   108
Acquisitions. *See* Mergers and
   acquisitions
   due diligence, absence, 39
   opportunism, 140
   promises, checking, 45
Activist shareholders, impact,
   161
Akzo Nobel, 161
Alfa Group
   arbitration connection, 58
   boycott, 57–58
Alphabet (Google), 162
American International
   Group (AIG), fall, 8
American Public Medical
   Group, 106

Anchoring/adjusting,
   avoidance, 123
AOL, digital progress
   (failure), 115
AOL Time Warner merger,
   46–48, 73
Apple
   operations, optimization,
   13
Apple, gross earnings/
   earnings per share,
   12–13
Arguments, quantity/quality
   (contrast), 125
Asset purchase, 141
Assets
   domestic assets, foreign
      purchase (tension),
      163–164
   marketing, 88
   transfer taxes, absence, 142
Assets under management
   (AUM), 166
ATM fee (NYC), history, 23
ATM networks, installation,
   23–24

ATM transactions,
    processing, 27
AT&T/T-Mobile
    case study, 110–115
    regulatory discussions, 112
    stock purchase agreement,
        112
Autonomy, culture, 80

Bailey, David, 99
Bain Consulting, 166
Bank
    branches, combination, 15
    funding position, 92
    liquidity, disappearance,
        108
    separation, 88
    stock price, pressure,
        89–90
Banker ego, collateral
    damage, 129
Banking
    experience, quality, 28
    presence, establishment, 14
Bank of America (BofA)
    accounting policies,
        changes, 108
    laws/regulations, changes,
        108
    seller, actions, 108
    shareholders, deal
        approval, 109
    support, 109
    terrorism/war, acts, 108

Bank of America (BofA),
    Merrill Lynch purchase,
        39, 44
    case study, 5–12, 106–110
    position, 10
Bank of America (BofA)
    Merrill, MAC clause,
        107–108
Bank of America
    (BofA)/Merrill, MAC
    Clause, 171–173
Bank of England
    HBOS support, 90–91
    lender of last resort facility,
        92
Bank of Scotland, Halifax
    (merger), 88–89
Bear Stearns
    collapse, prevention, 150
    debt obligations,
        repayment demand, 149
    examination, private equity
        firms usage, 149
    formalized procedures,
        employee resistance,
        151
    founding, 8
    liquidity crisis, 149
    mortgage-backed securities
        write-down, 149
    stockholders, anger,
        149–150
    terms, Board of Directors
        perspective, 150

Bear Stearns, J.P. Morgan
  purchase, 148–152
  culture, imposition, 151
  deal price, 150
  integration, speed, 151
Best practices, 76–84
Bharti Airtel, 64
Bidders, elimination, 128
Blank, Victor, 91–93
Bluff, usage, 123
Boards of directors, role, 14
Borrowers, revenue collapse,
  158
Bozeman, Dave, 140
Brand, importance
  (recognition), 142–143
Breakup fee, removal, 101
Brekke, Sigve, 63–64
Brightgoods, product launch,
  67
British Petroleum (BP),
  Deepwater Horizon
  disaster, 160
Brown, Gordon, 87, 91–92
Bucyrus International,
  Caterpillar acquisition
  announcement, 137
  approval process,
    establishment, 145–146
  background, 137–138
  brand retention, 143
  continuous learning, 148
  dealers, involvement, 144

deal, structuring, 141–142
distribution efficiency,
  143–144
divisions, grouping,
  140–141
employees, solidification,
  141
equipment customization,
  144
factory support, 144
financing, arrangement,
  145
integration, importance,
  146
legal/regulatory process,
  clarity, 146–147
overpayment, avoidance,
  147–148
post-sales support, 143
senior management roles,
  integration, 151
stock purchase, 141–142
strategic approach,
  138–140
technicians/field staff,
  employment, 144
Buffett, Warren, 97, 101
Burger King Restaurants, 21
Business
  deal skills, importance,
    167–168
  life-cycle, 82
  risk, increase, 157

Buyer post-closing, income
generation, 142
Buyer/seller
culture, review
(importance), 48
transition services,
establishment, 45

Cadbury
history, 98
Kraft purchase
case study, 96–101
deal, background, 98–99
takeover, 101
Cadbury, John, 98, 163
Capital
allocation, 166
arrangement, 122
excess, 167
expenditures, reduction, 60
inadequacy, 34
injection, 92
management, 28
Capstone project, assignation,
76
Case, Steven (resignation), 47
Caterpillar
acquisition (*See* Bucyrus
International)
counterparty status, 142
culture, understand-
ing/management,
144–145
economic harm, 138

equipment, sale, 143
Global Mining business,
executive office
accountability, 140
Integrated Manufacturing
Operations Division,
140
management, longer-term
view, 140
Mining Products Division,
141
Mining Sales and
Marketing Division, 141
mining sector offering,
complement/increase,
146–147
rational organizational
structure, maintenance,
140–141
stock purchase,
advantages/disadvantages,
142
Central Bureau of
Investigation (India),
corruption charges, 63
Central Europe, Telenor
operations, 55
Centralized approach, 80–81
issues, 81–82
management, 81
Change in control clause,
142
China
case study, 71–74

PowerPoint presentation, 72

Chuanzhi, Liu, 143

Collaboration, usage, 129

Collateralized debt obligations (CDOs), 7

Collateralized loan obligations (CLOs), 7

Comfort zone, exit, 84

Commerce Bank
ATM network, installation, 23–24
branches, location, 24–25
case study, 21–26
customer satisfaction, 22
customer service, focus, 25
growth, 22
Metro Bank, similarities, 27
organic growth, 23
traditions, 25
value proposition, clarity, 26
WOW (internal program), 25

Commercial driver's license (CDL), obtaining, 33

Company
culture, change, 27
long-term goals, 83
portfolio, investment, 165
post-closing, 164–165

project-driven approach, 146

Competition, analysis, 65

Competition Appeal Tribunal, complaint, 93

Competition Commission, intervention, 91

Concessions, 129

Conglomerates
pure play trend, 161–163
stocks, undervaluation, 163

Constituencies, pressure (increase), 159–160

Continuous learning, 148

Contract negotiation, conclusion, 128

Core business (distraction), foreign activities (impact), 66

Core customer deposits, impact, 27

Corporate senior management, role, 14

Corporate social responsibility, worries, 99–100

Corporate strategy, real estate ownership, 130

Corporate veil, exposure, 31, 32

Corus Steel, takeover, 68

Cost synergies, 46

Counterparty
  culture, understanding, 73
  motivations,
    understanding, 132
  status, 142
Cox, Dylan, 166
Critical infrastructure,
  importance, 164
Cross-border deals
  care, 84
  nationalism, increase,
    163–164
  oversight, requirement, 75
Cross-selling products,
  impact, 15
Cross-selling targets,
  achievement, 49
Culture
  blending, problems,
    151–152
  building, 28
  differences,
    sensitivity/awareness, 83
  diversity, valuation, 76
  ethics/accountability
    interface, 79
  examples, 78–79
  factors, 80
  impact, 45
  management, 144–145
  old-economy company,
    culture, 47–48
  review, importance, 48

  setting, 83
    ability, 78
  soft concept, 83
  understanding, 35,
    144–145
Curfman, Chris, 141
Customers
  protection, 142
  retail experience, 28

Daniels, Eric, 87, 91–92, 95
  leadership, 90
Darling, Alistair, 91, 92
Day-to-day management, 83
Deals
  closing, motivation, 128
  cross-border deals, 75, 84,
    163–164
  deal-making process,
    integration (connection),
    146
  exit, belief, 131
  momentum, 100
  motivations, 5
  post-deal period, 145
  rational organizational
    structure, usage, 140
  size, increase, 167
  skills, importance,
    167–168
  structuring, 141–142
  teams, success/celebration,
    127
  values, 166–167

Deal-specific issues,
  sensitivity, 43
Deal teams, importance,
  45–46
Debt
  agreements, protections,
    157–158
  cost/availability/terms, 157
  zombies, 157
Decentralized
  model/approach, 80
Decision making,
  improvement, 77
Deepwater Horizon
  explosion, BP reaction, 160
de Leon, Luis, 141
De-novo, 40, 53
Depreciation write-off, 142
Deutsche Telekom,
  representative
  appointment, 110
Diamond, Bob, 4
Dimon, Jamie, 149–151
Distractions, avoidance, 128
Distribution efficiency,
  143–144
Diversity, valuation, 76, 78
Dividend policy, 161
Dodd Frank (act),
  implementation, 108
Domestic assets, foreign
  purchase (tension),
  163–164

Dow Corning
  silicone breast implants,
    class-action lawsuits,
    31–32
Dow Corning, JV case study,
  30, 31–32
Dow Jones Industrial
  Average, closing (record),
  157
Downside risk, 94
Dry powder, 166
Due diligence, 122
  100-Day Plan, usage,
    44–45
  absence, 39
  acquisition promises,
    checking, 45
  buyer/seller, transition
    services (establishment),
    45
  completion, 139
  culture, impact, 45
  experts, hiring, 44
  integration professional,
    involvement, 44–45
  objectivity, maintenance,
    44
  process, improvement,
    43–46
  resources, redirection, 145
  responsibility, 43–44
  skills, 43
  time, allotment, 66

Due diligence *(Continued)*
  transition services,
    establishment, 45
Duhigg, Charles, 39

Eastern Europe, Telenor
    operations, 55
  expansion, 57–59
Economy
  longer-term view
    (Caterpillar), 140
  volatility, 159
Egos
  collateral damage, 129
  impact, 127
  reduction, 129
Einstein, Albert, 127
Electronic delivery, bank
    usage, 22
Elliott Management
    Company, Akzo Nobel
    position, 161
Employment agreements,
    continuation, 142
Enterprise Act of 2002, 93
Enthusiasm, impact, 139
Equifax, home equity line
    report, 158
European Union (EU), UK
    exit, 159
Europe, Telenor operations,
    55
Executive Committee, open
    floor plan, 80

Exit options, defining, 35
Experience, leverage,
    123–124
Exposure, management, 7

Facebook, pure-play
    company example, 162
Family-run business, tensions,
    83
Farimex, basis, 58
Federal Communications
    Commission (FCC), 113
Fee income, generation, 7
Financial crisis
  boom years, relationship,
    166
  debt zombie percentage,
    increase, 157
  impact, 137
Financial institutions, moral
    hazards, 9
Financial markets,
    maturation, 162
Financial projects, GE review,
    148
Financial results,
    consolidation, 82
Financial Services Authority
    (FSA), HBOS support,
    90–91
Financing, arrangement,
    145
First-time funds, popularity
    (increase), 167

First Union Corporation,
merger, 40
Ford, purchase, 67
Foreclosures, cycle, 158
Foreign Corrupt Practices
Act, 66
Foreign markets, presence, 53
Foreign subsidiaries, holding,
75
Frito-Lay (PepsiCo), 97

Genachowski, Julius, 113
General Electric (GE)
core competencies,
expansion, 53
diversity, valuation, 78
financial projections review,
148
metrics, 159
vision, 159
General partner, 165
Geopolitical risk, increase,
157
Georgia State University, 5
Germany, foreign takeover
sensitivity, 163–164
Global confectionery leader,
creation, 98–99
Global economy, Merrill
Lynch failure (impact), 44
Golden West Financial
high-return, risk-averse
strategy, 40
losses, potential, 41

mortgages, addition, 42
operations, problems, 48
pick a payment loan, 42
Quick Qualifier program,
42
S&P500 financial index,
performance
(comparison), 42
Wachovia purchase, 40–46
Goldman Sachs, 9
core competencies,
expansion, 53
survival, 11
Goodwin, Fred, 4, 126–127
Google, diversification, 162
Government, bailout, 94
Great Recession, 89, 108
impact, 11
Greenberg, Alan, 151
Gross domestic product
(GDP)
growth, tracking, 138
shifts, 138
Growth
high-return, risk-averse
strategy, 40
M&A usage, 12–13

Halifax, Bank of Scotland
(merger), 88–89
Hayward, Tony, 160
HBOS
balance sheet,
complications, 89

HBOS (*Continued*)
government bailout, 90–91
history, 88–90
Lloyds bailout, 95
Lloyds TSB, merger, 87
merger
speculation, 91
timeline, 90–93
moral hazard, 94
mortgage book, risk, 89
shareholders, price offer, 91
stakeholders, confusion,
94–95
support, 90–91
toxic assets exposure,
89–90
Hill, Vernon, 21–26
Historic failure, root causes,
159
Homes, median sales price
(increase), 158
Honesty, usage, 128–129
Horizontal mergers, 14–16
Hornby, Andy, 91
Horrell, Jonathan, 99–100
Housing market bubble,
impact, 158

IBM personal computer
division, Lenovo
acquisition, 143
Income generation, 142
Indemnitor, role/impact, 125
India
economic attractiveness,
60
Telenor entry, 62
Industry-specific events, 107
Integration
deal-making process,
connection, 146
importance, 146
Integration professional,
involvement, 44–45
Intercompany transactions,
82
Interest payments, deferral,
158
Interests, misalignment,
29–30
Internal cross-selling targets,
achievement, 49
Internal rate of return (IRR),
3, 14
International assignments,
77
Investment
guidance, 45–46
presentation, 78
IPO, consideration, 83

Jaguar Land Rover, takeover,
68
Japan
case study, 74–76
cross-border deal, oversight
(requirement), 75
Job cuts, worries, 99

Johnson & Johnson (J&J)
  conglomerate example,
    161–162
  takeover, 12
Joint ventures (JVs)
  case study, 32–34
  cessation, 30
  controlling parties,
    identification, 30
  flexibility, 30–31
  interests, misalignment,
    29–30
  liability, 30
  limited liability, 31
  management distraction,
    30
  patience, requirement,
    35–36
  Telenor/Unitech, 61–63
  usage, 29–31
J.P. Morgan
  culture, imposition, 151
  leverage, 151
  purchase (*See* Bear Stearns)
JP Morgan Chase, Bear
  Stearns sale, 8

Khosrowshahi, Dara, 168
Kraft
  bids, increase, 98–99
  breakup fee, removal,
    101
  Cadbury merger, 96–101,
    163

corporate social
  responsibility, worries,
    99–100
deal momentum, 100
history, 96–98
job cuts, worries, 99
purchase, case study,
    96–101
Kraft, James L., 97
Kuka, 164
Kyivstar Wireless, Telenor
  ownership stake, 57

Land Rover, Tata purchase,
    68
Laws, changes, 108
Legal process, clarity,
    146–147
Lehman Brothers
  bankruptcy filing, 87, 108
  founding/bankruptcy, 8–9
Lender of last resort facility
  (Bank of England), 92
Lenders, proceeds collection,
    157–158
Lenovo acquisition, 143
Lenovo Pride Day, 143
Leverage
  creation, 131–132
  usage, 128, 131–132
Lewis, Ken, 5, 9–11, 44,
    109–110
  Banker of the Year award,
    6

LGBTQ community, employees, 78
Liability, impact, 107
Lifecycle management, 61
Limited liability, 31
Limited partners (LPs), 165–166
Liquidity crisis (Bear Stearns), 149
Listening, ability/willingness, 127
Lloyds Banking Group (LBG), 88
Lloyds Bank, Trustee Savings Banks (combination), 90
Lloyds HBOS
    case study, 87–96
    merger, 88, 93–94
    short-term focus, long-term focus (contrast), 95
Lloyds TSB
    financial position, enhancement, 92–93
    HBOS, merger, 87
    history, 90
Local geography, awareness, 29
Logos, change, 142
Long-term success, 145
Loss-making contract, entry, 106
Low-cost customer deposits, access, 27

Macdonald, Margo, 91
Makarenko, Victor, 57–58
Management
    centralized approach, impact, 82
    distraction, 30
Management teams
    distractions, 54
    interaction, 45–46
    success, 167–168
Mandelson, Peter, 93
Market response, 100–101
Market share, 40
Marstand, Rob, 157
Master negotiator, role, 125
Material Adverse Change (MAC), 105–108
    AT&T clause, 114
    invocation, failure, 110
Material Adverse Change (MAC) Clause, 169
    impact, 11–12
McDonald, Margo, 96
McGrath, Rita Gunther, 48
McMoll, Hugh (retirement), 5
Mergers and acquisitions (M&As)
    activity, 58–59
        dampening, 163
    approach, 3
    approval process, establishment, 145–146
    context, 78–79

deals
  effort, 124–125
  motivations, 5
discouragement, 25
diversification, 6
failure, determination,
  144–145
international expansion, 64
market
  pressure, 158
  size, 129
negotiation
  honesty, usage, 128–129
  personal contest,
    avoidance, 130
  purchase price,
    importance, 133
opportunistic approach,
  139
prices, increase, 166–167
private equity, impact,
  165–167
process, minority positions,
  57
standalone M&A
  committee,
  establishment, 145
strategic approach, 139
strategies, 61, 64
strategy, development,
  167–168
success
  determination, 144–145
  risks, 27

temptation, 53
transactions
  due diligence skills,
    43
  government involvement,
    trend, 88
  usage, 12–14
Merrill Lynch
  acquisition, 39, 44
    case study, 5–12
  losses, 108–109
  merger agreement, 109
  toxic assets, 110
  write-down, 8
Metro Bank
  case study, 26–29
  Commerce Bank,
    similarities, 27
Midea Group Co., 164
Moffett, Craig, 115
Moore, Paul, 89
Moral hazard, 94
Morgan Stanley, 9
  survival, 11
Mortgage-backed securities,
  Bear Stearns write-down,
  149
Mortgage payments, making,
  158
Mortgages
  addition, 42
  lenders, aggressiveness,
    148

Motivations, understanding, 132
Mutual gain, usage, 130–131

Nabisco Brands, R.J. Reynolds (merger), 97
Natural disaster, occurrence, 107
Negotiations
  ability, 121–122
  anchoring/adjusting, avoidance, 123
  closing, motivation, 128
  collaboration, usage, 129
  concessions, 129
  distractions, avoidance, 128
  ego, reduction, 129–130
  embarrassment, avoidance, 129
  feedback, 131–132
  honesty, usage, 128–129
  issues, focus, 124–125
  leverage
    creation, 131–132
    usage, 131–132
  listening, ability/willingness, 127–128
  motivations, understanding, 132
  mutual gain, 130–131
  patience, 126–127
    personal contest, avoidance, 130
    perspective, 123–124
      loss, ease, 124–125, 129
    practices, 124–133
    preparation, importance, 132–133
    sensitivity, 129
    success, reason, 125–126
Net operating loss carryforwards (NOLs), 142
Nordic countries, Telenor operations, 55
North Carolina National Bank, 5

Oberhelman, Doug, 138, 146–147
Objectives, clarity, 35
Objectivity, maintenance, 44
Old-economy company, culture, 47–48
O'Neal, Stan (replacement), 8
Operating skills, emphasis (increase), 164–165
Opportunism, presence, 140
Opportunistic approach, 139
Organization
  building, 76
  structure, type (selection), 83
Overpayment, avoidance, 147–148

Overseas
  expansion, M&A usage
    (risks), 53–54
  presence, building, 54

Pannon, 57
Parent company, clone
  (purchase), 81
Partnerships
  building, 73
  usage, 29–31
Party, knowledge, 35
Patience, requirement,
  35–36, 126–127
Paulson, Henry, 39,
  109–110, 148
Peltz, Nelson, 97
PepsiCo, 97
Personality profiling, 45–46
Philip Morris, Nabisco
  Holdings (addition), 97
Pick a payment loan (Golden
  West), 42
Piggy bank, 158
PIK toggle note, 157–158
Plaza Hotel, strategic assets,
  74
Political instability, 96
Post-closing integration,
  164–165
Post-deal period, 145
Post-deal workshops, 148
Post-integration workshops,
  148

Post-sales support, 143, 144
PPG, takeover, 161
Practices, commonality, 81
Pre-close
  negotiation/structure,
    importance, 164–165
Premium, award (absence),
  28
Preparation, importance,
  132–133
Prequin Alternative Asset
  Research, 165
Presence, establishment, 13
Private equity (PE)
  asset class, capital
    allocation, 166
  firms, fund raising success,
    166
  impact, 165–167
  industry, firm entries
    (increase), 167
  internal rate of return,
    average, 165–166
Problem solving, M&A
  (usage), 13–14
Product knowledge,
  awareness, 29
Project-driven approach, 146
Project-oriented
  organizations, workshops,
    148
Property, bidding process,
  122–123

Psychometric testing, 45–46
Purchase price, importance, 133
Pure play
    company, example, 162
    conglomerate trend, 161–163

Qualitative factors, dependence, 48
Quick Qualifier program (Golden West), 42
Quinn, Bob, 113

Rational organizational structure, maintenance, 140–141
Real estate
    costs, reduction, 15
    house tour, 131
Rebranding, tendency, 142–143
Recession
    housing market bubble, impact, 158
    impact, 137
    prediction, ability, 138
Regulations, changes, 108
Regulatory changes, 65
Regulatory process, clarity, 146–147
Renminbi
    (RMB)-denominated fund, setup, 73

Renminbi
    (RMB)-denominated private equity fund, establishment, 71
Renminbi (RMB) fund, 73
Reporting structure, selection, 78–79
Reputational risk, 65–66
Revenue streams, projection, 139
Revenue synergies
    achievement, 48
    care, 46
    driver, 49
Risk
    downside risk, 94
    identification, 39
    new paradigm, 7
    post-close, 45
R.J. Reynolds, Nabisco Brands (merger), 97
RJR Nabisco, corporate target, 97
Rosenfeld, Irene, 97
Royal Bank of Scotland (RBS), ABN AMRO
    acquisition, 3, 126–127
    case study, 4–5
Royal Bank of Scotland (RBS), value (decline), 92

Sales
    process, initiation, 122
    volatility, 138

Salespeople, Associates title, 79

Sandler, Herbert/Marion, 41

Saving face, concept, 77

Schneiderman, Eric T., 113

Seeking Alpha (Marstand), 157

Seller
actions, 108
protection, negotiation, 124–125

Senior management team
evaluation, difficulty, 29
failure, 49–50

Shareholders
activist shareholders, impact, 161
value, Welsh perspective, 160

Shareholders/analysts, attention, 65

Short-term success, 145

Shwartz, Alan, 150

Simulator training, 33

Skill set, comparison, 82

"Stability of the Financial System," addition, 93

Stakeholders, confusion, 94–95

Standalone M&A committee, establishment, 145

Standardization, synergy delivery (balance), 81

Standard & Poor's 500 (S&P500) financial index (performance), Golden West (comparison), 42

Standard practice, term, 107

Stock market value, loss, 108

Stock purchase, 141–142
advantages/disadvantages, 142

Stock transfer, tax payments (buyer avoidance), 142

St. Petersburg, wireless cell phone licenses, 57

Strategic approach, importance, 138–140

Strategic rationale, outline, 139–140

Stressed sales, cycle, 158

Stumpf, John, 48, 49

Subprime borrowers, terms, 148

Subprime mortgages, 6
investment bank exposures, 148

Success
change, maximization, 140
stories, contrast, 152

Supply chain, components (purchase), 16

Synergies, 15, 31
cost synergies, 46
delivery, standardization (balance), 81

Synergies (*Continued*)
 driving, 81
 revenue synergies, 46
Synthes, Johnson & Johnson
 takeover, 12
Systematic risk
 addition, 9
 elimination, 7

Tag lines, change, 142
Target companies
 buyer potential, 101
 function, 105
Target employees,
 consideration, 78–79
Target management team,
 adjustment, 82
Tata Consultancy Services,
 67–68
Tata purchase, 67–68
Tax basis, lower level,
 142
Tax liabilities, depreciation
 write-off, 142
Tax payments, buyer
 avoidance, 142
Tax structures, complexity,
 164
Telenor
 Asia operation, 59–61
 competition, analysis, 65
 Eastern Europe expansion,
  57–59
 entry barriers, 60

global strategy, 56–57
initiation, 55
lawsuits (Moscow), 58
low-cost operational
 model, 60
M&A international
 expansion, 64–65
management
 methods/marketing
 techniques, 61
minority positions, 57
mistakes, education, 65
operations, focus, 55
regulatory changes, 65
regulatory environment,
 opportunities, 59–60
reputational risk, 65–66
revenues, geographical
 mix, 56
risks, 65
shareholder concerns, 62
shareholders/analysts,
 attention, 65
share price, decline, 62
Telenor Group
 India entry, 63
 subscribers, addition, 59
Telenor JV, usage, 54
Telenor/Unitech
 joint venture, 61–63
  postmortem
   examination, 63–64
 negative reactions, 62

Telenor/Unitech, merger,
54–56
Telenor v. Kyivstar, 58
Terrorism, acts, 108
Tetley Tea, Tata purchase,
67–68
Thain, John, 8, 39, 44
Think Pad brand name,
Lenovo usage, 143
Third parties, protection,
142
Thompson, Ken, 41
Thomson Reuters Data,
AT&T deal examination,
114
Thrift franchise, conversion,
41
Time Warner Center, 9
Time Warner, merger. *See*
AOL Time Warner merger
T-Mobile/AT&T, case study,
110–115
T-Mobile, wireless spectrum
(transfer), 111–112
Trade-bait list, 132
Traditions, 25
Transfer taxes, absence,
142
Transition services,
establishment, 45
Trinity Foundation, MAC,
107
Trinity
International/American

Public Media Group, MAC
Clause, 169
Trust, culture, 80
Trustee Savings Banks (TSB),
Lloyds Bank
(combination), 90

Uber, 168
Uncertainty
introduction, 23
reduction, 16
Unicor, services (launch), 62
Union agreements,
continuation, 142
Unitech Group, startup
mobile operator, 56
Unitech/Telenor, merger. *See*
Telenor/Unitech
Unitech Wireless, 56
India deal, 63–64
United Technologies, core
competencies (expansion),
53
Unusual practice, term, 107
URS WellCom, VimpelCom
acquisition, 57
U.S. credit card debt, level,
157
U.S. Federal Reserve,
bailouts, 8

Value
addition, JV (impact),
30–31

Value (*Continued*)
  creation, core customer
    deposits (impact), 27
  proposition, clarity, 26
Vendors, protection, 142
Venture capital firms, fund
  raising success, 166
Verizon, 111
  bid, case study, 115–116
Vertical acquisition, 15–16
Vertical mergers, 14–16
VimpelCom
  arbitration, 58
  management proposal, 57
Volvo, purchase, 67

Wachovia Corporation
  acquisition/merger, 40–46
    deal, approval/risks, 41
  due diligence, 43
  formation, 40
  Wells Fargo purchase,
    48–50

Walden, Marni, 116
War, acts, 108
Wealth, shareholder loss, 95
Wells Fargo
  acquisition, 48–50
  postmortem report,
    49–50
Welsh, Jack, 159–160
White knight, 151
Working hours, flexibility,
  78
WOW (Commerce Bank
  internal program),
  25
Wunning, Steve, 140

Yahoo
  MAC language, leverage,
    116
  Verizon bid, case study,
    115–116

Zypries, Brigitte, 164